PRAISE FOR
IMPROVING WITH AGE

"God has numbered our days and we're still here b̶ ... ̶urpose
for us is not finished (Eph. 2:10). Stuart and ̶I̶'̶l̶l̶ ... *̶h̶ Age*
will not only help you make the mos̶t̶ ... ̶vant
to hear God's words, 'Well done ...

Cofou̶ ... ̶nternational
Author, teacher . ... ̶rer of Stuart and Jill

"In *Improving with Age*, the Briscoes don't just tell Christian seniors to live with optimism; they pack it with illustrations from their own lives to show how they can tackle life with enthusiasm and zest and make invaluable contributions to their families, churches, and society."

—Dan Brownell
Editor of *Today's Christian Living*

"Jill and Stuart Briscoe are living giants of our time. They have gone the distance—modeling for us marriage, parenting, grandparenting and pastoring, while keeping pace with our ever-changing times. I am thrilled that they have now written these important lessons on this valuable season of life."

—Mark Foreman
Pastor of North Coast Calvary Chapel
Author of *Wholly Jesus*

"*Improving with Age* is a timely reminder that those of us who are growing older are desperately needed in our families, our churches and society at large. Those who are retired from their vocations must realize that God has a future for them, not just in heaven but also on earth, even as they anticipate the challenges of old age. I know of no couple more qualified to write this book than the Briscoes, who have modeled continuous service for the Lord well beyond what we generally call the retirement age. I hope many thousands read these pages and find that old age can be welcomed, knowing that God has meaningful tasks for us to do."

—Dr. Erwin W. Lutzer
Senior Pastor of The Moody Church, Chicago

"Some people might call the years after retirement 'The Golden Years.' Although this might be true for some, for far too many few experiences are really golden. This is, in part, because they haven't done a new assessment of who they have become, and further, they have failed to fully realize their potential for what could be an amazingly long season of life. The church can help. In their book *Improving with Age* the Briscoes help the reader discover possibilities and value for a new and exciting season. They also encourage Christian communities to seriously expand ministry to and with seniors, especially giving attention to equipping them for productive Kingdom building. In giving themselves for the mission of God more fully, many seniors will truly discover these years are indeed golden."

—Dr. Norb and Jackie Oesch
Founders of the Pastoral Leadership Institute

"My longtime friends Stuart and Jill Briscoe really know how to enjoy their golden years, and they do it in a way that significantly enlarges their eternal estate. While most seniors kick back, retire and step out of ministry, the Briscoes are moving toward life's finish line with joyful exuberance and consummate purpose. And the best part is, they've sketched out a practical road map for the rest of us seniors in their remarkable new book *Improving with Age*. If senior living is getting you down, this book will truly help you live onward and upward!"

—Joni Eareckson Tada
Joni and Friends International Disability Center

"Many 'successfully aging Christian heroes' are left unchallenged by today's church. I highly recommend *Improving with Age*, in which Stuart and Jill Briscoe explore the unique Kingdom value of every Christian at or near retirement age."

—Ward Tanneberg
Author of *Redeeming Grace*
President Emeritus, CASA 50+ Network

IMPROVING
WITH AGE

God's Plan for Getting Older and Better

Stuart and Jill Briscoe

CLC
PUBLICATIONS
Fort Washington, PA 19034

Improving with Age
Published by CLC Publications

U.S.A.
P.O. Box 1449, Fort Washington, PA 19034

UNITED KINGDOM
CLC International (UK)
Unit 5, Glendale Avenue, Sandycroft, Flintshire, CH5 2QP

ISBN (trade paper): 978-1-61958-207-1
ISBN (e-book): 978-1-61958-208-8

CONTENTS

Part 3: Aging: Older People in the Contemporary Church

FOREWORD

During many years of conference ministry, my wife and I have always rejoiced when the schedule teamed up with Stuart and Jill Briscoe. Why? Well, for one thing, they are fun to be with and there's always lots of laughter. But even more, they know how to blend biblical truth with practical counsel that has grown out of their own ministry experiences.

I like that. It's ministry fresh and alive and enlightening.

This book was written just the way they minister in public. It's packed with lots of "church facts" and ideas that I wish I had known years ago when I was pastoring and trying to bridge the so-called "generation gap." Now I'm among the "old folks" and, believe me, I need all the help I can get. From their studies and personal experience, Stuart and Jill have keen insight into the dynamics of change, the unique problems of old folks, the goals of the younger crowd, and the approaches we can take to minimize conflict and maintain unity and diversity in the church.

First and foremost, *Improving with Age* is for all the older folks who want to make the most of their senior years. But it's also ideal for church members and leaders who want to build bridges and not walls—who want to enjoy the younger generation and encourage them without sounding like the wicked witch of the west. I also strongly recommend this book to all ministers and church leaders who want unity, variety and maturity in the church family for young and old and those in between.

As I look back on my early years of pastoring, I thank God for the adults whose examples, prayers and mentoring skills helped make the congregation one happy family. Had I read this book sooner, they probably would have been happier!

But enough! Enjoyment and enrichment are awaiting you, so start reading!

Warren W. Wiersbe

Teacher, speaker and author of

Too Soon To Quit

ACKNOWLEDGMENTS

Many people have contributed to this book, not a few of whom had no idea a book was being written. Chief among them were and are the wonderful seniors with whom we have worked in Elmbrook Church and around the world.

Rosalyn Staples, the pastor of our original seniors' ministry, deserves special mention. Her wise counsel, compassionate service, wry humor and prayer-bathed ministry were a blessing to all of us.

Dave Almack and the staff of CLC Ministries proved once again to be Christian publishers in every sense of the term.

Becky English brought her singular skills and assiduous attention to detail to bear on our work and improved it immensely.

Shelly Esser, the editor of *Just Between Us* magazine and a dear friend and colleague of long-standing, provided invaluable counsel throughout the project and insisted on being positive when I wondered at times if the book would ever get written or would ever be read!

Rhea Briscoe, our daughter-in-law and personal assistant, gets us where we need to be when we need to be there and ensures that everything—including writing books—gets done when necessary.

Lastly, we are so grateful to our friend Dr. Warren Wiersbe for taking a break from his prodigious production of great reading material to write kind words about this effort, which pales beside his.

To all the above, we are more grateful than we can express on this page.

INTRODUCTION

For many years I, Stuart, have awakened on my birthday (when I've remembered it!) to ask with great puzzlement, "How can someone as young as me be as old as this?" Now that I'm well past my eightieth birthday, my age begs the question, "How can this be?" and the answer comes loudly and clearly: by God's grace!

Of course, that is the answer to every question dealing with our surviving and prospering in this challenging world. It relates to everybody, regardless of how many years we have completed. Robert Robinson (1735–1790) was only twenty-two years of age when he wrote the well-known hymn "Come Thou Fount of Every Blessing." Despite his relative youth, he had packed a lot of dissolute living into his years, enough to recognize the wonders of God's forgiving grace and tender mercies. He wrote:

> Come, Thou Fount of every blessing,
> Tune my heart to sing Thy grace;
> Streams of mercy, never ceasing,
> Call for songs of loudest praise.
> Teach me some melodious sonnet,
> Sung by flaming tongues above.
> Praise the mount! I'm fixed upon it,
> Mount of Thy redeeming love.

Here I raise my Ebenezer;
Here by Thy great help I've come.[1]

He was reflecting on the words of Samuel the prophet, who, after a great victory for Israel following some ignominious defeats attributable to Israel's disobedience, raised a stone called Ebenezer. The highly visible monument was erected to commemorate the Lord's work in the lives of His people, and it signified, "Thus far the LORD has helped us" (1 Sam. 7:12).

That, frankly, is my story! I have suffered personal defeats attributable to disobedience and a lack of faith—the two common enemies of the disciple's life—but where I have demonstrated obedience and trust, expectation and delight, I have seen tangible evidences of God's gracious "help." This word "Ebenezer," incidentally, should not be interpreted as meaning that the Lord is a benevolent assistant who is always on call; rather, He is the One who enables, provides, equips and supports.

The problem for some of us is that we sometimes fail to recognize the Lord's hand in the help that comes our way; we therefore omit giving Him the praise that is His due. For example, I see His "help" in the family I was born into; in the protection I received in irresponsible youthful days; in my survival in the Marines; in the gift of a wife called Jill; in three supportive, encouraging kids and their families; in robust health and energy over many decades; in an American church family that took a small family of Brits and their golden retriever into their hearts; in countless friends, sisters and brothers from around the world who have poured their lives into ours; and so on. I raise my Ebenezer!

By the way, the correct term for someone in their eighties is "octogenarian," which I once assumed meant one who subsists on a diet of octopus the way a vegetarian subsists purely on vegetables. How wise we become in our old age!

A word of explanation about this book: Jill and I wanted to produce something dealing with a subject of universal interest—aging. Aging is a process in which everybody is involved from birth. It's not reserved for the aged. People of all ages are older than they used to be—that's called aging!

This aging process starts at birth and continues until death, and it involves a lot of living in between. In our more benevolent moments, we excuse challenging young people by saying, "They're only acting their age; they'll grow up." Later we celebrate their coming of age. Before long they arrive at middle age, and before we know it, retirement age. When we ourselves reach this milestone, we become more aware of aging, although it has been weaving its quiet way through our lives all along. Eventually, people refer to us as aged, until one day we pass away, having lived to "a good old age" (Gen. 25:8).

Call it what you will, it's aging. It happens to everybody, it's perfectly normal, and life should be lived to the full at each stage. Jill and I wanted to write something that could encourage people who are experiencing the aging process. This encouragement is found primarily in the pages of Scripture, where we discover that the aging process is perfectly normal and that it has some very definite upsides in addition to its well-documented downsides. Moreover, Scripture teaches us much about embracing life in all its stages, which is another way of talking about functioning in the aging process.

Accordingly, I have written the teaching sections of the book, and Jill has brought her abundant creativity to bear on my efforts by producing additional material to help in group studies, to deepen personal applications, and to implement in community the things we learn through studying "improving with age."

We hoped to produce something that can be used not only on an individual basis but also as a tool for small-group study and discussion. If you aren't part of a small group, why not invite some friends or family over to read and discuss this material together? After all, people who are aging usually recognize the need for fellowship and welcome opportunities to enjoy it. We hope that this book will prove helpful in this regard.

Finally, we recognize that the church has a pivotal role to play not only in human development (aging!) but also in the challenges and opportunities facing an aging population. In our view, the modern church doesn't appear to always recognize the vast potential of the aging church population. The unique skills, experiences and resources of these individuals need to be harnessed. Church ministries for older people should not be focused solely on caring for the aged but also on mobilizing those who are full of energy, ideas and experience yet have been parked on the sidelines of church life. While it is understandable and necessary for churches to focus on reaching the rising generations, we must not overlook the spiritual needs of the huge numbers of aging people outside the church. We must not fail to encourage and equip our aging saints to invest their mature years in vigorous ministries reaching out to their contemporaries who, after all, are the ones closest to eternity!

PART ONE

AGING: MORE THAN GROWING OLD

Gray hair is a crown of glory;
it is gained in a righteous life.

Proverbs 16:31, ESV

1

AGING HAPPENS, AND YOU CAN'T STOP IT!

In the interest of full disclosure, I need to tell you that I was born in 1930—more than eighty years ago. As far as I know, I am still in good health and have lots to do. My energy, while diminished, is still in evidence. I have worthwhile objectives to pursue, and I am lovingly supported, encouraged, provoked and corrected by "the wife of [my] youth" (Prov. 5:18). I am surrounded by mature, godly, adult children and hordes of grandkids who love and perplex me in equal measure. I have more friends and colleagues than I deserve. In short, I'm blessed.

Many of my contemporaries are not as blessed as I am. For them, aging is not happening as easily as it appears to be for me at present. I hope to write with them in mind; I also write for those who are blessed like me. Theologian and educator Dr. Vernon Grounds famously pointed out that aging means "diminishing," and he was right. When older men get together to tell war stories, we often give the inescapable impression, "The older we are, the better we were." Memories fade, details get revised and stories improve with every telling, so our revisionist personal history is under-standable if not entirely forgivable! The reality is that we look fondly on the past because it reminds us of the days before we became diminished. Talking about it, frequently in embellished tones, helps us deal with the painful loss of energy, opportunity and influence that aging brings. Poet Thomas Campbell said it best: "Distance lends enchant-ment to the view."[1]

Having said that, a large number of seniors have no in-tention of being called seniors or of behaving like seniors. Because of advances in medical health, an increased aware-ness of self-destructive behaviors and improved nutrition, many seniors are actively making a mockery of the birth date on their driver's license. In addition, the generation of the baby boomers, having reinvented each stage of life as they approached it, are now redefining and reinventing ag-ing and retiring too. I must admit that I make no objection when a bright, young airline employee checks my identity and intones, "This says that you're over eighty; you don't look a day over sixty!"

My wife, Jill, quotes the following with great glee:

> In the dim and distant past,
> When life's tempo wasn't fast,
> Grandma used to sit and knit,
> Crochet, tat and babysit.
>
> When the kids were in a jam
> They could always count on Gram.
> In the days of gracious living
> Grandma was the gal for giving.

Grandma now is at the gym,
Exercising to keep slim.
She's out touring with a bunch,
Taking clients out to lunch.

All her days are in a whirl,
Driving north to ski and curl.
Nothing now can block or stop her,
Now that Grandma's off her rocker.[2]

Well-meaning friends have sent me books that I "absolutely need to read." Most of them, including such masterpieces as *70 Ways to Beat 70* and *Younger Next Year*, promise, if not the reversal of the aging process, at least the opportunity to deny it with some degree of justification. Diet advertisements show remarkable pictures of flabby fifty-five-year-old men entitled "before" morphed into buff sixty-year-old men entitled "after." Their female equivalents feature wrinkle-free, radiant beauties proudly announcing, "Sixty-five is the new thirty-five!"

Now, I agree that if we can diminish diminishing, let's do it. If we can prolong good health and vigor and active, productive living and look like a million dollars while doing it, let's go for it. But the following two realities must be faced: Aging is inevitable—it's part of being human. And aging means diminishing—it will happen. Denying these realities doesn't help; ignoring them is not smart. We're called to confront them, embrace them and live in the reality of them. When we respond to these realities rather than react against them, aging is full of surprises.

We are aware that cheeses and fine wine improve with age, but it may be a surprise for some of us to realize that humans can and should improve with age too. I have some positive things to say about aging, while taking into account the difficulties that are inevitably part of the process.

For Personal Reflection and Group Discussion

Points to Ponder

- We look fondly on the past because it reminds us of the days before we became diminished.
- Thomas Campbell said it best: "Distance lends enchantment to the view."
- The following two realities must be faced: Aging is inevitable—it's part of being human. And aging means diminishing—it will happen.
- Aging is full of surprises.

Discuss/Journal/Pray

1. Spend some time reflecting on the Points to Ponder.
2. Can we diminish diminishing?
3. Have you been spending too much time wishing things were the way they used to be?
4. Is it hard for you to embrace life in all its stages?
5. Add to the realities of aging mentioned in this chapter. Aging is_____

_____

_____

A Personal Note from Jill

I was leaving the house to speak to the seniors at our church. "Where are you going?" asked my husband. "I'm going to speak to our seniors," I replied happily. "I love talking to them!" My husband glanced up from his work and said briefly, "'Them' is 'us,' Jill!" I stopped abruptly and pondered the impossible. I had arrived!

Have you arrived? Are you "them" or "us"?

2

AGING MEANS DIMINISHING

Let's start in an unusual place—the ancient book of Ecclesiastes, particularly 12:1–8. Ecclesiastes is a puzzling book that has given, and continues to give, challenges to many people. Its twelfth chapter amplifies advice introduced to young people in chapter 11, and while it encourages them to have a good time, it also warns them that eventually "God will bring [them] into judgment" (11:9), so they should "remember [their] Creator in the days of [their] youth" (12:1). In other words, young people should use common sense. Better yet, they should gain godly wisdom. Another way to say it is that while young people will sow their wild oats, smart ones will recognize that sowing wild oats means reaping wild oats—and that is not productive living. They should wise up— the sooner the better!

The author of Ecclesiastes, "Qoheleth" (a name that Derek Kidner says is "untranslatable"[1]), further warns young people that the day will come when "the dust returns to the ground it came from, and the spirit returns to God who gave it" (12:7). Young people should never forget that God created them and that eventually their bodies will return to the dust and their spirit will return to God.

You're probably wondering what this sobering advice about youth has to do with aging. In verses 1–8, the writer contrasts the carefree days of youth with "days of trouble" and pleasureless years. Even a cursory reading of these verses shows that Qoheleth is referring to aging. Theologians don't always agree on the interpretative method to be used for this passage, but the text seems to me to be a picture of advancing years. So let's read Ecclesiastes 12:1–8 as an ancient depiction of life in all its ages and stages. Warning: we may have to use a little, or maybe a lot of, imagination!

The author starts out in verse 2 by comparing aging to gloomy, stormy weather. (Having spent half my life in the north of England, I know precisely what he is talking about; that area only has two seasons—winter and the second week in August! But back to Ecclesiastes.) Our author then goes into a detailed description of aging in verses 3–5. He says that "keepers of the house tremble" (referencing shaky hands), "strong men stoop" (wobbly legs), "grinders . . . are few" (dental problems), "windows grow dim" (cataracts), "the sound of grinding fades" (hearing loss), "people rise up at the sound of birds" (insomnia), they "are afraid of heights" (acrophobia) "and of dangers in the streets" (agoraphobia), "the almond tree blossoms" (hair turning white), "the grasshopper drags itself along" (the get-up-and-go got up and went) and "desire no longer is stirred" (no interpretation necessary). And after aging, gracefully or otherwise, eternity beckons. The "silver cord is severed" (12:6) and "mourners go about the streets" (12:5).

This isn't a pretty picture, but it isn't inaccurate either. Depressing? Discouraging? Disappointing? For some people, it's all of the above!

A pastor friend told me of his experiences ministering in a southern Sunshine State that is well-known for its high population of retired people. He urged me to pack my bags and join him to work in what he called a mission field of lonely, embittered, disappointed older people. He said, "They whittle away their time isolated from family, playing cards, drinking too much, complaining and becoming addicted to prescription drugs." These people have lost all sense of relevance and purpose but are clinging to their lives with a touch of desperation—not because they feel their lives are so full of meaning but because the alternative offered is, in their view, uncertainty at best and grim possibility at worst.

Such people need to be reminded of something the author of Ecclesiastes certainly did not forget: however diminished a human being may become, he or she is still a unique creation whom God the Creator chose to create. For Qoheleth, aging was not a story of life falling apart, plans coming to naught or life's meaninglessness finally being exposed. He addressed aging very realistically in a context that insisted that an aging person is nothing less than an integral part of divine creation. Remember, the whole poem—for such it is—is predicated on the need to "remember [our] Creator" before it is too late. The author explicitly talks of death not as the final inevitable insult (at worst) or as a merciful release from meaninglessness (at best) but as a spiritual return to the Creator, as well as a physical dissolution of the body: "The dust returns to the ground it came from, and the spirit returns to God who gave it" (Eccles. 12:7). We need to explore this further.

For Personal Reflection and Group Discussion

Points to Ponder

- The aging person is nothing less than an integral part of divine creation.
- However diminished a human being may become, he or she is still a unique creation whom God the Creator chose to create.

Discuss/Journal/Pray

1. Spend some time reflecting on the Points to Ponder.
2. Read Ecclesiastes 12 out loud. The teacher exhorts us, "Remember your Creator in the days of your youth, before the days of trouble come" (12:1), and again, "Remember him—before . . . the dust returns to the ground it came from, and the spirit returns to God who gave it" (12:6–7).
3. Spend some time contemplating one thing about God that you learned in your youth.
4. Was there a point in your life at which you forgot to remember?
5. Have the "days of trouble" drawn you closer to God or driven you from Him?
6. If you think about it, everyone is aging. Has your get-up-and-go got up and gone?

7. Do you feel as though you have lost your sense of relevance? If so, begin praying for God to show you His purpose for you in this season of your life.

A Personal Note from Jill

Here are some ideas to *restart* or *refresh* your daily devotional life. As R.A. Torrey used to say, the best way to begin is to begin.[2] Choose one idea from the list below!

- Call a Christian friend to talk.
- Visit the church of your choice (again).
- Buy a modern translation of the Bible and read a chapter every day.
- Take a walk outside in God's creation (His "cathedral") and worship Him.
- Listen to some worship music.
- Ask God to give you a waking thought each morning.
- Invite a few friends over for coffee or tea and discuss this chapter.

3

CREATED!

During my days as a senior pastor, I worked with a number of younger men and women. When one of them, Bob, gave his first talk at the church, he was eager for me to hear and critique his message. I looked forward to listening to what he had to say. But I cringed as he announced his topic: "God Don't Make No Junk." He certainly gained the attention of the congregation, but I'm afraid my critique began with his title! In response to his assertion that "God don't make no junk," I told him, "God don't use no bad grammar neither!" Bob's presentation was good, his message correct, his intentions right on, but his title hardly did justice to the topic.

However, aging people who would cringe with me need to be reminded that my young friend was right! "God don't make no junk," even though on occasion we begin to wonder if He did in our case. Realism insists that we are not what we used to be, but realistic reckoning also notes that we weren't made the way we are—we became this way!

There are days when we feel as if we are no longer needed, respected or useful. "Junk" is probably not the word we would choose even in our darkest moments, but feelings of insignificance can take over. In moments like this, we need to remember that we have a Creator, which means that we were created. The word "created" points to an intentional, purposeful, meaningful action of God that resulted in our existence and that continues to operate throughout our life's stages and into our later years.

If God doesn't make junk, then what precisely did He make when He made you and me? Details of the wonderful truth that we are intentionally created are graphically portrayed in some of the Bible's opening words: "The LORD God formed a man from the dust of the ground and breathed into his nostrils the breath of life, and the man became a living being" (Gen. 2:7). (Note that the generic word translated "man" in this context denotes humanity rather than masculinity and therefore includes "woman.") The operative words in this verse are "dust" and "breath" (the word "breath" in Hebrew also means "spirit"), and the result of these two coming together is a "living being" (literally "soul").

In the case of man, he was created alongside the animals, which were made out of materials similar to those from which he was created. Whether or not we want to admit it, an affinity clearly exists between animals and mankind! Moreover, man and animals came into existence because God called on the "land [to] produce living creatures," or animals (1:24), while the same God formed man from "the dust of the ground." There isn't a lot of difference between land and dust. Yet while we physically bear unmistakable affinities to the animal kingdom, we are utterly different from it. What's the difference? According to the Scriptures, that which separates humanity from the animal kingdom is the fact that, unlike everything else in the created order, mankind was created "in the image of God" (Gen. 1:27). This fascinating term can be applied in numerous ways, but surely it means that when God made us, He made special beings capable of a deep relationship with the Creator. It is in the spiritual dimension of our being that human uniqueness lies.

While "the image of God" is never explained in detail, we do know that man has the ability to hear from God (see, for example, Gen. 3:9). We know that as a rational, emotional and volitional creature, man can understand what God communicates, and that as a spiritual being, he is capable of behaving appropriately. This understanding of God, His person and His purposes informs a person's will, which in turn is designed to control his often unruly and erratic emotions. The result is life lived in loving, trustful obedience. This is the kind of life for which mankind was uniquely created—a life in union with the God who made us, the God who is the source and meaning of life.

As the hard business of living takes its toll, it is the spiritual dimension of life that often wears out first. Doubts, disappointments, injustices and abuses accumulate over the years. We may even begin to question God's goodness and then resent His inaction and turn away from His presence, losing all sense of His grace and purpose for our lives. "Junk" feelings take over. This is too often the lot of those who are aging, but it is emphatically not what God intended.

For Personal Reflection and Group Discussion

Points to Ponder

- "God don't make no junk."
- We are not the way we ought to be.
- We were intentionally created for a purpose.
- Our uniqueness as people lies in our spirituality.
- God is the source and the meaning of life.
- As the hard business of living takes its toll, it is the spiritual dimension of life that often wears out first. Doubts, disappointments, injustices and abuses accumulate over the years. We may even begin to question God's goodness and then resent His inaction and turn away from His presence, losing all sense of His grace and purpose for our lives.

Discuss/Journal/Pray

1. Spend some time reflecting on the Points to Ponder.
2. Do you ever wonder why God created you?
3. Are you happy with your body, personality and abilities?
4. Are you ever tempted to feel like junk?
5. Write or talk to God about this. If appropriate, share your thoughts with a group.
6. Write out Psalm 139:16. Memorize this verse. Think about it. Talk to the Lord about it. *Believe* it!
7. Pray Psalm 139:23–24 for yourself and others.

A Personal Note from Jill

Read Psalm 139. Everyone is searching for meaning and purpose. Which verses of this psalm are pertinent to you or to someone you know? Think of a way, or choose a way below, to share a verse from this psalm with someone.

- Write a card.
- Make a phone call.
- Take a friend to coffee.
- Invite some of your grandkids or your neighbors to come over for ice cream and discussion.
- Use this "Personal Note from Jill" with any group.

4

OUTWARDLY AND INWARDLY

G od did not create mankind and then leave us to ourselves to figure out why we'd been made and what we were supposed to do. God's intentions for man were stated unambiguously: man would live fruitfully, purposefully and significantly, free from worries or cares. His work would be profoundly important and beneficial, abounding in variety, with endless possibilities for exploration, experimentation, development and discovery.

Man's *mind* would be stretched as he sought to grasp the immensity and the complexity of what he ruled over. His *emotions* would be ravished by the beauty and the wonder of it all. His *will* would be exercised every time he walked past the tree that had been declared off-limits; and he would be required to obediently stifle his innate curiosity and accept that God, in His wisdom, did not want him looking into matters of good and evil independently of God Himself. In other words, man was to enjoy the fullness of his humanity—to be what God intended man to be.

But by the same token, God warned that should man repudiate his creaturely dependence on the Creator (the essence of sin), the relationship would be shattered, and man's experience of union with the Creator would be terminated. Separated from the source of life itself, man would experience death (see Gen. 2:16–17). This death, we discover from the Scriptures, involves physical, spiritual, and eternal estrangement and separation from God.

Recently I sat at my desk working on my computer— a reading lamp casting a golden glow on my desk, music playing quietly in the background, the air conditioner whirring away and the coffee machine gurgling in the corner of the room. Suddenly, with a violent crash of thunder, the lights went out, the computer went black, the music died, the air conditioner ground to a halt and the coffee stopped percolating. In an instant the machines had been cut off from their source of energy. The loss of this vital force demonstrated itself in a variety of ways depending on the machine, but the cause was the same in each instance. So it is with mankind's separation from God. It shows up in a thousand and one different ways.

If we think of mankind as having been created to be governed by God's presence, through His Spirit in our spirit, we can perhaps catch a glimpse of the glorious potential of humanity fully living in ideal surroundings. This is how God created man, male and female, in the beginning, and as with everything else that He created, He pronounced it good (see 1:31). But then when man rejected God's benevolent rule, the Spirit of God was removed from within him, and a completely new scenario was introduced. This is no longer creation; this is the Fall. This is not the world as it was intended to be; it is the world as it has become!

At this point we should ask ourselves, what then became of man in this fallen world? What became the new governing principle of his existence? What made man tick after the Fall? As C.S. Lewis poignantly remarked, "A new species, never made by God, had sinned itself into existence."[1] This "new species," no longer alive with the life of God's Spirit, slid into the death of existence governed by factors other than spiritual: factors such as our affinity with the animals, factors such as our being related to dust.

Instincts and impulses appeared, and men and women began to behave badly. In no time at all, the human condition deteriorated, society started to fragment and the world as we now know it was born. Our "dustness" became apparent as purely chemical factors started to rule in us, ungoverned by the Spirit of God, and as our physicality began to show signs of wear and tear. The body, made by God to be the dwelling place of His Spirit but now bereft of His presence, began to experience pain and suffering, disease and dying. Life that displayed both residual evidence of created beauty and new evidence of fallen ugliness became normative. Aging was introduced.

Whether we are aware of it or not, the process of aging is going on; and the older we are, the more apparent it becomes. In the process of aging, which is a kind of slow dying, our systems wind down and our organs wear out. When organs cease to work, death occurs. Eventually, aging catches up with us all.

So how should we look at aging? Try this approach. *Creation*: I was made by God for a purpose in His created order.

Fall: Like the rest of humanity, I did not live in an appropriate relationship with God and accordingly became alienated from God, my source of life. Physical death was not instantaneous, but a slow process of dying—demonstrated by aging, among other things—took over. This is not at all what God intended. *Redemption*: This is about God looking at His fallen world, deciding He wanted it back, and taking steps to intervene and roll back the Fall's consequences. And if aging, a slow dying, is part of the Fall's fallout, then God has a role to play in the aging process.

The apostle Paul knew a few things about the difficulties of aging. He struggled with a mysterious illness that he called his "thorn in [the] flesh" (2 Cor. 12:7). For this he sought relief and healing, but he never experienced it. That must have been as excruciating as it was disappointing. There can be little doubt, in addition, that years of arduous travel, imprisonments, shipwrecks, stoning and beatings took a massive toll on Paul's body. Paul was well-acquainted with aches and pains as well as with the emotional toll of being deserted by some and maligned and misrepresented by others. He saw churches that he had planted torn apart and saw those whom he had nurtured in the faith turn away from the Lord.

But Paul's attitude was remarkable. He pressed on. He persisted. On one occasion, in the midst of a really bad situation, he twice insisted, "We do not lose heart," and he added by way of explanation, "Though outwardly we are wasting away, yet inwardly we are being renewed day by day" (4:16). By "outwardly" he was presumably talking about the physical realities that he was dealing with; but when he turned his attention "inwardly," he was focused on his spiritual life.

The physical dimension was clearly in eclipse, but the spiritual dimension was equally clearly in ascendancy. It is on this point that I want to focus. Without in any way ignoring or downplaying the outward aspects of aging, which can be onerous or worse, we need to focus on the inward aspects that promise blessing and enrichment, hope and joy. It is in the experiencing of these things that we begin to improve with age!

Consider this possibility: Could it be that wasting away physically and being renewed spiritually are equal and opposite realities? Could both these processes be preludes to, and reminders of, the physical return to dust and the spiritual return to the Creator? Are we living now in processes that will be completed later in eternity? If so, this casts a fascinating light on the subject of aging—a special kind of aging that involves physical diminishing and spiritual developing. This positive development offers hope and encouragement en route to ultimate fulfillment in the presence of the Creator, Redeemer and lover of our souls. But more than that, it is a destination in His carefully prepared "new heaven" and "new earth" (Rev. 21:1), where He promises that "He will wipe every tear from [our] eyes. There will be no more death or mourning or crying or pain, for the old order of things has passed away" (21:4).

But I'm getting ahead of myself. Before this grand finale to life on earth as we know it and the grand unveiling of glory as we cannot even imagine it, there is still a lot of living to be done with the dual theme in focus: outwardly we are wasting away; inwardly we are being renewed day by day. It's the day-by-day renewal that we must now explore.

For Personal Reflection and Group Discussion

Points to Ponder

- C.S. Lewis poignantly remarked, "A new species, never made by God, had sinned itself into existence."
- Life, at times displaying both residual evidences of created beauty and fallen ugliness, became normative. Aging as we experience it was introduced.
- Whether we are aware of it or not, the process of aging is going on; and the older we are, the more apparent it becomes. Eventually aging catches up with us all.
- The physical dimension was clearly in eclipse, but the spiritual dimension was equally clearly in ascendancy.
- Could it be that wasting away physically and being renewed spiritually are equal and opposite realities? Are both these processes preludes to, and reminders of, the physical return to dust and the spiritual return to the Creator? Are we living now in processes that will be completed later in eternity?

Discuss/Journal/Pray

1. Spend some time reflecting on the Points to Ponder.
2. Read Second Corinthians 5:1. Does this illustration remind you of aging? In what way?
3. Read Second Corinthians 4:16. Consider whether or not you agree with this statement: "Could it be that physically wasting away and spiritual renewal are equal and opposite realities?"

4. Think of some examples of beauty and ugliness living in close proximity to each other, and consider how this helps explain aging.

5. How does the reality that you are inwardly being renewed even though you are outwardly wasting away give you hope?

6. Pray for some aging friends who may not know Christ. Also pray for missionaries in difficult places who are taking these truths to people who have never heard them before.

A Personal Note from Jill

However many ways we have experienced our bodies wasting away, let's use the time we have left to invite people into conversations about "a building from God, an eternal house in heaven" that awaits those who know Jesus (2 Cor. 5:1). One way to do this could be to send them a booklet like John Stott's *Becoming a Christian*. This little booklet was used to lead me to faith in Christ while a student at Cambridge.

5

RENEWED DAY BY DAY

Our God, the Creator of heaven and earth, was not about to leave His wrecked creation in its fallen state. As soon as He dealt with His original erring children, He immediately promised that the seed of the woman would crush Satan's head but would be mortally wounded in the process. This was the first indication of God's plan to counter the consequences of sin and death (see Gen. 3:15). Progressively, over the centuries, God revealed more of His plan. The seed of the woman would be God's Messiah, a King who would sit on an eternal throne. He would suffer grievously and be killed, but His body would not "see decay" (Acts 2:31). Piece by piece the progressive revelation was unfolded until finally Christ Jesus was born, grew up, lived and was crucified (the promised mortal wounding). Then He was raised from the dead on the third day, and the confusing prophecies were fulfilled.

In the great event of the resurrection, God defeated death and introduced something entirely new—resurrection life! Fast-forward to Revelation 21:5, and you will read, "He who was seated on the throne said, 'I am making everything new!'" As he heard those words spoken, the aged apostle John "saw 'a new heaven and a new earth,' for the first heaven and the first earth had passed away" (Rev. 21:1). God was revealing the end of the story—the ultimate reversal of the Fall.

God is actively making all things new; He is in the renewal business. It started with raising Jesus from the dead; it will end when this old created order of ours is made into a new heaven and a new earth. But what, if anything, is going on during the centuries-long interval between Jesus' resurrection and the promised ultimate new creation? The answer is a resounding, "God is mightily at work in this interval in which we are living, and what He is doing intimately involves us."

Paul described what is going on in detail: "We know that the whole creation has been groaning as in the pains of childbirth right up to the present time. Not only so, but we ourselves, who have the firstfruits of the Spirit, groan inwardly as we wait eagerly for . . . the redemption of our bodies" (Rom. 8:22–23). I do not want to be dogmatic and state that hurricanes, tornadoes, tsunamis, volcanic eruptions, earthquakes, droughts, monsoons and raging wildfires are evidences of creation's groaning. Neither would I insist that our inward groaning is limited to the pains and troubles of aging. But these things certainly illustrate the point that everything is in need of renewal, which God is actively bringing about!

Writing more specifically, Paul stated in another place that the Lord Jesus Christ, "who, by the power that enables him to bring everything under his control, will transform our lowly bodies so that they will be like his glorious body" (Phil. 3:21). One day our old dust bodies that give us aches and pains will experience a resurrection of their own; they will be renewed, and we will inhabit a body similar to the one Jesus occupied after His resurrection. I assume that means that our new bodies will be as ideally suited to the new heaven and the new earth as our present bodies, however dysfunctional they may have become over time, were remarkably fitted for life on planet earth.

You might be saying to yourself, *This sounds like pie in the sky for when you die, but I'm aging now!* Fair enough; but when we understand what God is doing, embrace what He has promised and trust that He will be faithful, fresh living hope is born again in our hearts, and we face life with renewed vigor and purpose.

But there is more!

For Personal Reflection and Group Discussion

Points to Ponder

- God is in the renewal business.
- Take heart; we are waiting for God to eventually do what He has promised to do, what Paul called "the redemption of our bodies."
- One day our old dust bodies that give us aches and pains will experience a resurrection of their own and will be renewed. Then we will inhabit a body similar to the one Jesus occupied after His resurrection.

Discuss/Journal/Pray

1. Spend some time reflecting on the Points to Ponder.
2. Romans 8:22 says, "The whole creation has been

groaning." Does that inward groaning remind you of some of the aches and pains of aging? How so?

3. Read Philippians 3:21. Would you say that you are in the process of transformation—becoming like Jesus?

4. It is the inward work of the Holy Spirit that accomplishes our transformation and is responsible for the improving in our aging in the deepest recesses of our humanity. How does this bring you encouragement?

5. Read Second Corinthians 5:17 and 3:18. Which verse brings you the most joy?

A Personal Note from Jill

One of my life lessons is that the older we get, the more we tend to live in denial concerning our age. We never think we are old, but apparently everyone else does.

In the not-too-distant past, on a freezing Wisconsin winter night as my husband and I left our church, I slipped on the ice in the parking lot and knocked myself out. As I came to, I heard a young man on his cell phone calling for an ambulance and saying, "An elderly woman has just fallen in the parking lot." I thought, *Isn't that amazing! Another woman fell at exactly the same time as me!*

God helps us to stay young on the inside; yes, He does! Just ask Him!

6

FRESH AND FLOURISHING

The aging process, as we all know, has a termination point—except for those who will be alive at Christ's return (see 1 Thess. 4:13–18). Death is the terminus. But in the case of Jesus, death was also the prelude to resurrection, and it will be for the believer as well.

Never forget what Paul wrote on this theme: "If Christ is in you, your body is dead because of sin, yet your spirit is alive because of righteousness. And if the Spirit of him who raised Jesus from the dead is living in you, he who raised Christ from the dead will also give life to your mortal bodies through his Spirit, who lives in you" (Rom. 8:10–11).[1] There's a connection here. The Spirit who is at work right now in believers' lives will not complete His work until, at the resurrection, He gives life to our mortal bodies. So He is busy in time and will complete His work in eternity—a continuum of grace.

I love the vibrant expression "your spirit is alive," and I'd like to explore it further since it gets right to the heart of being renewed day by day—or improving with age!

Four main biblical texts employ the word "renew," and they all focus more or less on the same theme: "renewed day by day" (2 Cor. 4:16); "renewed in knowledge in the image of its Creator" (Col. 3:10); "transformed by the renewing of your mind" (Rom. 12:2); "renewal by the Holy Spirit" (Titus 3:5). A different but similar Greek word is used in Ephesians 4:23 and is translated, "made new [renewed] in the attitude [literally "spirit"] of your minds." Paul was saying that renewal is the work of the Holy Spirit in the human spirit, particularly referencing how the Spirit imparts knowledge to the human mind. In another context Paul referred to believers "being transformed into his [the Lord's] image with ever-increasing glory" as they "contemplate [or reflect] the Lord's glory" (2 Cor. 3:18).

Transformation comes as believers recognize that they are new creations in Christ and acknowledge that, at the time they embraced Christ as Savior, they took "off [their] old self with its practices and . . . put on the new self, which is being renewed" (Col. 3:9–10). This is much like taking off dirty gardening clothes after working among the vegetables, showering and putting on clean clothes to eat supper. One aspect of this taking off and putting on is the taking off of old attitudes and the putting on of totally new attitudes born out of a love for Christ and a desire to know Him better. When we do this, hunger for contemplating His beauty, hearing His Word and discovering His truth is born in us. The Spirit obliges by giving us renewed knowledge through our careful study of God's self-revelation in Christ and His Word. You may remember that we noted at the beginning of chapter 4 that God reveals truth to the *mind*, which then informs the *will* in order that it may control the *emotions*, and the result is God-honoring behavior.

Aging people tend to spend more and more time in the doctor's office, where they meet many contemporaries who are in varying stages of wasting away. When you go yourself, listen carefully to the conversations around you. Understandably, people have many sad stories of disappointment and worry, medication and discomfort. Imagine the contribution that a believer who is being renewed in spirit could bring to such an assembled company—reflecting a quiet confidence and steadfast hope as a result of having been refreshed that morning in contemplation of the Word and in a fresh experience of the Spirit's grace in his or her heart and mind. Believers' bodies, like everybody else's, are giving them grief, but their spirits are being renewed—and it shows.

I was nine years old when the Second World War broke out. Living in the north of England—close to shipyards, airfields, artillery ranges, and even prisoner of war camps—many charged activities went on around me. Young men from all over the British Empire came to my hometown for training with the Royal Air Force. As many of them were believers, they found their way to my parents' home for rest and fellowship, a little home comfort, and my mother's endless love and support.

One man, a captain in the Royal Artillery, a career military officer, stands out in my mind. He had grown up in difficult circumstances and had joined the army as an underage cadet.

There was something magnetic about Captain May. He was buoyant, consistent, positive, gracious, interesting and interested, unfailingly polite and incorrigibly cheerful. But he had one disconcerting habit. He often stayed overnight in our home; and he would come down to breakfast, smile broadly and say to me, "Good morning, Stuart. What is your best thought so far today?" When he first asked for my best thought, I froze, but as time went on, I recognized that he genuinely wanted to know what was going on in my life and wished to stimulate me to think good thoughts and express them cogently. He began to show me the importance of Scripture in his life. He taught me to think through what I was reading, to meditate during the day on what had been impressed on my mind, and to share freely and naturally the things I believed God had shown me that day.

Captain May was fresh. He was daily and continually renewed. It showed, and I wanted what he had! He was by no means an elderly person, but he wonderfully exemplified the psalmist's picture of being inwardly renewed: "The righteous will flourish like a palm tree, they will grow like a cedar of Lebanon; planted in the house of the Lord, they will flourish in the courts of our God. They will still bear fruit in old age, they will stay fresh and green, proclaiming 'The Lord is upright'" (Ps. 92:12–15). That's what it means to be renewed—even when outwardly we're wasting away.

For Personal Reflection and Group Discussion

Points to Ponder

- I love the vibrant expression "your spirit is alive," because it gets right to the heart of being renewed day by day—or improving with age!

- God reveals truth to the *mind*, which then informs the *will* in order that it may control the *emotions*, and the result is God-honoring behavior.
- Captain May began to show me the importance of Scripture in his life. He taught me to think through what I was reading, to meditate during the day on what had been impressed on my mind, and to share freely and naturally the things I believed God had shown me that day. Captain May was fresh. He was daily and continually renewed.

Discuss/Journal/Pray

1. Spend some time reflecting on the Points to Ponder.
2. Look up the following key verses that speak of renewal: Romans 12:2; 2 Corinthians 4:16; Ephesians 4:23; Colossians 3:10; Titus 3:5.
3. Summarize in your own words what these verses say about renewal while aging. Respond in prayer.
4. How can you show the importance of Scripture in your life? How can it daily renew you?

A Personal Note from Jill

Do you know of someone who is sick in the hospital or worried about his or her health or about aging? Perhaps sending that person a card with a summary of your thoughts about renewal would encourage him or her.

Do you have a plan to daily read the Scriptures? Regularly reading the Word is one of the best ways to experience renewal. Why not decide to read through the gospel of Mark—perhaps a chapter each day? As you read, do the following:

- Ask the text questions.
- Look for answers in the passage.
- Try asking these sorts of questions: *Who* is in this story? *When* did this happen? *Why* did the people react like this? *What* happened next?
- Journal as you read.
- Then pray (have a conversation with God) about what you have discovered.
- Capture a thought from each story or passage in your journal; then think of someone to pass it on to.

7

LOOK GOOD, FEEL GOOD

I logged onto my computer to start writing about improving with age a couple of days ago and was greeted with the smiling face of Christie Brinkley. In case you're not sure who this lady is, she has been a supermodel for a long time. According to the blurb under the picture, she is now over fifty and doesn't look like it, and that was apparently newsworthy. Frankly, I have little or no recollection of fifty, but for women whose main claim to fame is their physical beauty, I suppose fifty is *big!* I also understand that many people look at Ms. Brinkley and want to know her secrets, for they too would like to thwart the ravages of time and look as good as she does.

King Canute I of England was also a lord of Denmark and the king of Norway and of Scotland. He was so powerful that he imagined he could command the sea to stop rising and it would obey him. He therefore moved his throne to the beach, only to discover to his chagrin that the sea was not his to command. He could not roll back the ocean. Many stubborn people learn the hard way by taking a tumble. King Canute learned by getting a soaking. Having learned his lesson, King Canute could teach modern people a thing or two about trying to tell aging to stop: there are limits to earth-lings' abilities, and stopping aging is not within those limits.[1]

It is noteworthy that the noble king, after getting his feet and legs wet, not only admitted that he was wrong but proclaimed that earthly power has limits and that the power to rule the waves belonged only to the One who had created them. As a result, he never again wore his crown but ordered that it should be placed above a crucifix on which the Lord of heaven and earth hung. Those who resist the incursions of age should admit their limits as the king did, and they should acknowledge that their times are held safely in the hands of Him who, as the King of kings, rules the cosmos and all that is in it. Our aging is not ours to worry about but His to improve as the times take their toll.

Nevertheless, we are physical, which is why we have such a great interest in physical appearance. We notice this interest in the way old friends greet each other after an absence:

"Wow, you look good."

"Yeah, I feel good."

"You look good too."

"I feel good."

This conversation can go on for quite a long time, circling round and round looking good and feeling good, so in the interest of saving time on such occasions, let me give you a conversation stopper. Simply insert a simple question: "Are you being good and doing good?"

In our culture, inordinate emphasis is placed on physical appearance, sometimes to the detriment of concern for spiritual well-being. We are more focused on looking good than on being good and doing good! Those in the faith community who worry about this tendency remind us that Paul said, "I strike a blow to my body and make it my slave so that after I have preached to others, I myself will not be disqualified for the prize" (1 Cor. 9:27).

On the other hand, undue emphasis on downplaying physical appearance has led to various types of Christian asceticism that have not necessarily brought about spiritual growth and maturity. We need to steer between the extremes of decorating the body on the one hand and disparaging it on the other. Paul, as usual, had a healthy balance. He wrote, concerning the Christian's body in the context of eventual resurrection, "The body that is sown is perishable, it is raised imperishable; it is sown in dishonor, it is raised in glory; it is sown in weakness, it is raised in power; it is sown a natural body, it is raised a spiritual body" (15:42–44). In other words, while our bodies can be used as "an instrument of wickedness" (Rom. 6:13) and therefore require disciplined monitoring (Paul's "blow" to the body), they are not intrinsically evil. They may be "perishable," "dishonored," "weak" and "natural," but our bodies are still candidates for transformation and participation in the new heavens and the new earth. Therefore, they should be cared for, nourished, prized and presented "as a living sacrifice, holy and pleasing to God" (12:1) while functioning as "an instrument of righteousness" (6:13).

Accordingly, we should not worship our physical attributes or find our identity in them, but neither should we disregard or neglect them. "Dying" and "decaying" are not nice words, but they belong in our story. However, they are far from being the whole story; dying and decaying are preludes to destiny, and the believer's destiny includes a glorified body. Our bodies may be wasting away, but they have an eternal future nevertheless!

Some friends of mine try to maintain a right balance in the way they view their bodies by inserting little notes to themselves in the place where they are most likely to be focused on their bodies—the bathroom mirror. I'm not suggesting that we should be confronted by "Prepare to meet thy God" every time we shave or "It is appointed unto man once to die, after that the judgment" while applying makeup. But reading "Offer your bodies as a living sacrifice, holy and pleasing to God—this is your true and proper worship" (Rom. 12:1) while brushing our teeth may encourage us to take good care of this "offering" by perfecting our smile while recognizing that our worship makes God smile. That's what matters!

For Personal Reflection and Group Discussion

Points to Ponder

- Many people look at Christie Brinkley and want to know her secrets, for they too would like to thwart the ravages of time and look as good as she does.
- In our culture, inordinate emphasis is placed on physical appearance, sometimes to the detriment of concern for spiritual well-being.

- We don't worship our physical attributes or find our identity in them, but neither do we disregard or neglect them. Our bodies may be wasting away, but they have an eternal future nevertheless!
- "Dying" and "decaying" are not nice words, but dying and decaying are preludes to destiny, and the believer's destiny includes a glorified body.

Discuss/Journal/Pray

1. Spend some time reflecting on the Points to Ponder.
2. Would you, as a Christian, say that you have more interest in looking good, being good or doing good?
3. Read Romans 12:1–2. Verse 1 says, "Offer your bodies as a living sacrifice." What does this mean?
4. How can we put so much focus on the physical that we neglect concern for our spiritual well-being?
5. Pray about these things.

A Personal Note from Jill

Where do you find your identity? God made you on purpose, you know! Let me share a poem with you:

> You made me on purpose
> You knit me together,
> You promised Your presence
> Come wind or come weather.
> I'm the work of Your fingers,
> You say I'm Your "poem,"
> You made me on purpose,
> And You're leading me home.

IMPROVING WITH AGE

I need to stop running
And hold myself still,
My heart needs to listen
As You tell me Your will.
Though the road may be rough
And the way may be wild,
You made me on purpose,
And I know I'm Your child.

So broken and contrite,
I'm sorry for me;
For my fears and my phobias
That are so plain to see.
But it's never too late
To trust and obey
And walk home together
And hear Your voice say:

I made you on purpose,
You'll be Mine in that hour
When I make up My jewels
By My Almighty power!
So come live in the Glory
And hear angels' praise,
For I made you on purpose
For Eternity's days.[2]

PART TWO

AGING: WHAT TO DO WHILE IT HAPPENS

Age is not decay; it is the ripening, the swelling, of the fresh life within, that withers and bursts the husk.

—George MacDonald

8

MIRROR, MIRROR ON THE WALL

Snow White's stepmother was deeply attached to her talking mirror. She also appears to have had a fragile ego, for she repeatedly asked the mirror, "Mirror, mirror on the wall, who is the fairest of them all?" As long as the mirror assured the queen that she was the fairest of them all, everything was well; but when Snow White superseded her as the preeminent beauty in the land, there was trouble. Mirrors can stimulate self-absorption, feed pride, generate jealousy, and sometimes, in the case of aging people, they have been known to provoke memories of what used to be.

I saw an example of this when I recently had cataracts removed from both eyes. While waiting in the doctor's office, I was told about a lady who had had the same procedure. She had been ecstatic about the results. She had spoken excitedly of clearer vision, sharper focus, richer colors and other delights. But upon her first look in the mirror, she immediately had called the doctor to see if the procedure could be reversed!

The apostle Paul spoke of a mirror that kindled none of the self-focused attitudes listed above. In chapter 6, I mentioned Second Corinthians 3:18, which is sometimes translated as, "All of us . . . reflect the glory of the Lord" (NLT), and as, "We all, . . . beholding the glory of the Lord" (ESV). The original Greek word *katoptrizomenoi* (from *katoptron*, "mirror") means "to see something in a mirror."[1] In an ordinary mirror, the reflection is a reproduction of whomever is looking into it; Paul's mirror, however, doesn't reflect the person looking into it but rather the "glory of God in the face of Jesus Christ" (2 Cor. 4:6, ESV). So what is Paul beholding? Following the example of the earlier disciples, he is saying, in effect, "We have seen his glory, the glory of the one and only Son, who came from the Father, full of grace and truth" (John 1:14).

This priceless privilege was not limited to the original disciples and the Apostle to the Gentiles. Far from it! Paul specifically wrote that "we all" are involved. All have the opportunity to behold (or contemplate) and understand the glory of God, as reflected in the life and ministry of Jesus, because the Holy Spirit actively reveals, explains and applies to believers what they need to know from the gospel of Jesus. The result is progressive "transform[ation] into his image" (2 Cor. 3:18).

There's the clue. Being improved, renewed or transformed is synonymous with being changed into the likeness of Jesus. It's a process, and it's progressive. As it had a definite beginning, it also has an ultimate goal that will be realized in eternity. The aged apostle John explained it: "Dear friends, now we are children of God, and what we will be has not yet been made known. But we know that when Christ appears, we shall be like him, for we shall see him as he is." He added, "All who have this hope in him purify themselves, just as he is pure" (1 John 3:2–3).

To be transformed, we have to contemplate, read, mark, learn and inwardly digest the Scripture in which Christ, through whom the glory of God is seen, is revealed. Then the Spirit who inspired the Scriptures, whose "sword" is the Scriptures, and who resides in believers to interpret and implement the truth, can actively create an appetite for renewal in us. This stimulates our desire for the Word, which consistently imparts understanding to our slow hearts and minds and gently prompts us to and empowers us for obedience, trust, worship and rejoicing.

It's rather obvious, isn't it? The longer a person avails himself of the opportunity to contemplate Jesus—thus allowing the Spirit to apply His Word to our lives—the better the chance of transformation. In other words, the longer we live, the more mirror-gazing we can do; and the more we gaze, the more we transform. There's a real chance this will result in improving with age!

For Personal Reflection and Group Discussion

Points to Ponder

- The opportunity to contemplate the glory of God, as reflected in the life and ministry of Jesus, is available to us as we study the Scriptures. The Word is understandable because the Holy Spirit actively reveals, explains and applies what is recorded in the gospel of Jesus. We are then called to respond to what we know. The result is progressive transformation into the likeness of Jesus.

- To be transformed, we have to contemplate, read, mark, learn and inwardly digest the Scripture in which Christ, through whom the glory of God is seen, is revealed.
- The longer a person avails himself of the opportunity to contemplate Jesus—thus allowing the Spirit to apply His Word to our lives—the better the chance of transformation. In other words, there's a real chance this will result in improving with age!

Discuss/Journal/Pray

1. Spend some time reflecting on the Points to Ponder.
2. Take the above statements, think through them, and pray simply, "Lord help me to better understand the Holy Spirit's operation in my life and how He helps me improve with age." Then write this prayer out in your own words.
3. When we listen to Jesus' voice in Scripture, obey it, and use the pain that comes with aging to drive us nearer to God to experience His help, we are made more like Jesus. Then, in fact, we are able to use our hurts to share the comfort He gives us to comfort others. Read Second Corinthians 1:3–7. How can you comfort others?

A Personal Note from Jill

Why not set your clock to some unearthly hour and, when you wake, go to some unearthly place to talk to God about some earthly things? Why not go to the deep place where nobody goes and spend some time on the steps of your soul?[2] When you get there, be quiet for a while until all the noise in your headspace stops. Sometimes music helps. Then have a conversation. Afterward, maybe capture in writing your thoughts about your talk with God. Maybe leave a thank-you note on the steps outside God's front door.

Borrow my words and make them your prayer:

> Thank You for Your gift of Life and thank You for Your Spirit
> Thank You for Your gift of grace much more than I could merit.
> Thank You for the whispered words that made my soul stand still,
> Until I grasped Your message and began to know Your will.
> Thank You for the joys You've given in friends and family,
> And thank You for the sorrows too and life's realities.
> For there would be no mending if my heart had not been broken,
> And there would be no need that Your sweet Spirit's words be spoken.
>
> So thank You for the mending when our whole world falls apart,
> And thank You for Your nail-pierced hands that cradle riven hearts.
> Above all for the joy that's ours that only You bestow,
> The gift above all earthly gifts: Your risen life to know![3]

9

JESUS WASN'T ELDERLY

I have spoken much about the image of God, about being transformed into Christ's likeness, and about the work of the indwelling Spirit producing an inwardly maturing life while the physical body and external circumstances move in the opposite direction. By this time you may be thinking, *That's enough theory; now it's time for something practical!* I agree. I think it's time for us to explore what an aging person, becoming progressively like Christ, would actually look like in today's world.

Immediately we run into a problem, though, because Jesus was crucified and raised and returned to glory while still in His early thirties. Because He never had a chance to taste aging, we can't study an elderly Jesus. But Jesus certainly suffered, and, for a number of excruciating hours on the cross, He experienced dying. All His life, Jesus was confronted with the reality of His inevitable, imminent death, but He was never elderly.

However, we do know that the Spirit who empowered Jesus, the Son of Man, is the One who does His ancient work in our bodies and who transforms our earthly existence as the years roll by. We also know what is entailed in aging. There is no reason, then, that we cannot apply what we know of the real work of the Spirit to what we know of an aging person's realities.

Speaking of realities, I'd like to address the optimists and the pessimists among us. The former prefer to look at a situation and see the glass half-full, while their counterparts, viewing an identical situation, will often declare the glass half-empty. My wife frequently accuses me of looking at everything as if the glass is half-full. She goes even further and says that I am an incorrigible optimist and that my favorite expression is, "I don't anticipate any major difficulties." She has even promised to place on my tombstone the inscription: "Here lies Stuart Briscoe; he did not anticipate any major difficulties." Logically, my response to that is, "My dear, you are assuming that I'm going before you, but I'm not anticipating any major difficulties!" However, I insist that I do not regard the glass as either half-full or half-empty. I know full well that the top half is completely empty while the bottom half could not be fuller. In my view, "half-full" people are optimists, "half-empty" people are pessimists, and those who carefully observe, evaluate and give equal credence to what is actually happening in the top half and bottom half of the glass are realists.

So let's be realistic about aging. Some inveterate aging optimists exist, but I suspect that they are in the minority. They are easily recognizable. Possibly with the aid of nips and tucks and buffing and tanning—not to mention Botox and certainly the good fortune of having inherited good bones and better genes—they fail to look or act their age. They dress in the latest contemporary fashions although their best days belonged to a former era. They persist in playing age-defying games and driving death-defying automobiles (full disclosure: I drive a Mini Cooper). They are so busy being cool and having fun that they never cast a sideways glance at the passing years. Optimists, yes; realists, no.

Meanwhile, the pessimists focus almost entirely on their diminishing influence, the good old days, their medical coverage, domestic politics, and the numerous and deepening intractable international problems. They do not fail to bemoan today's youth and their music, dress and tattooing, which used to be associated with drunken sailors in faraway ports but now graces the bodies of supermodels. Less regularly are pessimists' lips graced with a word about the unique opportunities offered by their advancing years. A healthy dose of realism for them would go a long way.

Jill and I recently saw a great example of this kind of healthy realism on a spiritual-heritage tour in England. Among many other fascinating places, we visited the church where John Newton, a former slave-ship captain and the author of the all-time favorite hymn "Amazing Grace," was formerly the rector. We found a laminated copy of one of his quotations that beautifully spoke to the issue:

> I am not what I ought to be,
> I am not what I want to be,
> I am not what I hope to be;
> But by the grace of God
> I am not what I was.[1]

I have no idea how old John Newton was when he wrote those words, but I suspect he was speaking from the wisdom of age. I don't know, but the older I get, the more I too acknowledge the truth of these sentiments. "I am not what I hope to be" is a positive statement based realistically on the promises of God and on Newton's knowledge of the ongoing work of the Spirit. So is Newton's joyful and very realistic recognition that the old days were well behind him. There was no cause for triumphalism, however, for he knew that he had a long way to go. So do I! That's being realistic. I'm not the man I was, nor am I the finished object!

Now we can apply this to our understanding of the diminishing and improving trajectories that we have discussed. From a diminishing point of view, I am most certainly not the man I was! The prospect of seeing Jesus in His ascended glory and being changed into His likeness boggles my mind and realistically tells me, "You've got a long way to go Briscoe!" Let's look into what we can do while we realistically face the future.

For Personal Reflection and Group Discussion

Points to Ponder

- Jesus was crucified and raised and returned to glory while still in His early thirties. Because He never had a chance to taste aging, we can't study an elderly Jesus. But Jesus certainly suffered, and, for a number of excruciating hours on the cross, He experienced dying.

- Optimists prefer to look at a situation and see the glass half-full, while pessimists viewing an identical situation will often declare the glass half-empty.

- "Half-full" people are optimists, "half-empty" people are pessimists, and those who carefully observe, evaluate and give equal credence to what is actually happening in the top half and bottom half of the glass are realists.

Discuss/Journal/Pray

1. Spend some time reflecting on the Points to Ponder.
2. Having read this far, had you begun to think, *That's enough theory—now it's time for something practical?* Is biblical principle or practical advice more important? Why?
3. Are you an optimist or a pessimist? How does this affect your faith?
4. Are your prayers optimistic or pessimistic? If you are an optimist, try praying prayers of confession. If you are a pessimist, try praying prayers of praise.
5. What does it mean to be realistic about aging? (For example, should Stuart Briscoe be driving a Mini Cooper?)

A Personal Note from Jill

When aging, it's important to be realistic and to know yourself! Unlike my optimistic husband, I am a pessimist. I help myself by

- counting my blessings;
- looking back and remembering how God has answered my prayers; and
- praising Him for His presence in the pain that He allows in my life, because without it I would never have known His sufficiency.

What about you—how can you grow in this area of your aging? Make your own list to help yourself.

10

LET'S GET REAL

A few years ago, when my wife and I were both negotiating our seventies, we were invited to California to receive an award. We were not aware that we had done anything particularly noteworthy, but we accepted the invitation because the conveners of the conference had asked us to address the hundreds of church leaders committed to seniors' ministry who would be in attendance at the event.

On the flight there, my wife asked me, "What is this award for?" I was at a loss and so told her frankly, "For getting old, as far as I can tell." Then as an afterthought I added, "But getting old hardly warrants an award. All you do is stay alive, and it happens to you!" Now that's being realistic. Aging happens! Deny it, fight it, resist it, bemoan it, ignore it, but it will go on happening; and the longer you deny, fight, resist, bemoan or ignore it, the more it will happen and the older you'll get!

I think it was Jill's sixty-fifth birthday that caused her some heartache. Being a good husband, I tried to help her. I asked her if she thought she had been born at the right time, and she agreed that she had. I then inquired if she had been living at the right speed of 365 days per annum. After a little thought, she agreed that she had done that too. I assured her that, logically, if she was born at the right time and had been living at the right speed, she must have arrived at exactly the right age! She was unimpressed and retorted, "Your problem is that it is so long since you were sixty-five that you've forgotten what it feels like!" We were joking, of course, but there's truth to the premise that those who are born at the right time and who live at the only speed available to humans must, at any given time, be exactly the right age. I find that challenging, reassuring and totally realistic. I say to myself (which in itself can be a sign of something), *I am exactly the age I'm supposed to be. I'm right on schedule!*

Obviously, the relentless passage of time can be viewed as a negative. We often ruefully say, "Where has all the time gone? It seems like only yesterday that such and such a thing happened." We may even subscribe to Isaac Watts' old hymnal paraphrase of Psalm 90:

> Time, like an ever rolling stream,
> Bears all its sons away;
> They fly forgotten as a dream
> Dies at the opening day.[1]

There's no doubt that the passage of time is as relentless as an ever-flowing stream; and equally, there is no gainsaying the fact that as time goes by, people inevitably eventually pass away. A doctor friend told me one day, "Life has been proven to be 100 percent fatal." That's sobering; but, depending on how people prepare, it holds promise of something far better.

You may have heard of the funeral director who was seen placing a fork in the hand of a deceased lady immediately before he closed the casket. When asked about this, he said, "She left word in her will that her pastor had told her that life is the main course, but life after death is the dessert, and the best is yet to come. She wanted to be well prepared— hence the request to be armed with a fork." Shaky theology, but a great attitude! There's nothing shaky about Paul's great theological statement concerning what lies ahead for the believer: "'No eye has seen, no ear has heard, and no mind has imagined what God has prepared for those who love him.' But it was to us that God revealed these things by his Spirit" (1 Cor. 2:9–10, NLT).

Let's be real about this. Do you love the Lord and show it by a life of loving, trusting obedience? If so, then try a little exercise. Think of the most wonderful thing you have ever seen, the most beautiful sound you have ever heard, and the most mind-boggling concept you have ever imagined, and know that they all pale into insignificance compared to what lies beyond the grave after an inevitable death. The Spirit has taken steps to reveal the enormity of the future to us, not in detail but in principle, and we live in the glorious anticipation of experiencing all this by God's grace.

For Personal Reflection and Group Discussion

Points to Ponder

- Aging happens! Deny it, fight it, resist it, bemoan it, ignore it, but it will go on happening; and the longer you deny, fight, resist, bemoan or ignore it, the more it will happen and the older you get.

- I am exactly the age I'm supposed to be. I'm right on schedule.
- Life has been proven to be 100 percent fatal.

Discuss/Journal/Pray

1. Spend some time reflecting on the Points to Ponder.
2. Read Second Corinthians 5:1–10; then discuss:
   - How is our house in heaven described? (5:1)
   - What can we be confident about? (5:6–8)
   - What goals should we set in light of the above? (5:9–10)
   - How does this perspective help us as we age?

A Personal Note from Jill

Before my mother passed away, she indicated that she wished to be buried with my father in a beautiful country churchyard among graves dating back hundreds of years. I had the privilege of choosing the words that would be engraved on her tombstone. It gave me great comfort to be able to choose, "Absent from the body, present with the Lord."

I wrote this little poem to remind me of the hope of heaven:

HEAVEN

What place is this where rivers flow
And flowers bud and grasses grow?
Where birds compete to praise God's Son,
Where prayers are answered every one.

What place is this where minds released
From fear and phobia find peace?
Where constant joy is all I know,
Where God is everywhere I go,
Where I am overwhelmed to see
The face of Him who died for me![2]

11

SHAKY THEOLOGY

Since I brought up shaky theology, let me add a few thoughts on the subject. It seems logical to me that, as everybody knows that life ends in death and that the older we get, the nearer we are to that inevitability, people should give serious consideration to this topic. I don't mean that they should become obsessed with dying and emotionally paralyzed so they stop living to any great extent. But Ecclesiastes poignantly points out, "It is better to go to a house of mourning than to go to a house of feasting, for death is the destiny of everyone; the living should take this to heart" (Eccles. 7:2). I'm writing this early on the morning of January 1, and I would hazard a guess that far more people within ten miles of my home went to a party last night than to a funeral home. (I went to neither. I went to bed—that's called "aging"!)

I frequently meet people who avoid the subject of the possibility of life beyond the grave at all costs. Others assume that they will go to a better place, but they have no solid ground for their assumptions. Still others have embraced a Western brand of Eastern religion that makes the idea of reincarnation more appealing than it is in the original version. In the East, reincarnation basically says that if one dies and hasn't lived well, he or she will come back as someone or something inferior; but if a person does all right, he or she will return as a superior entity.[1] Western-style reincarnation assumes that everybody comes back better, regardless of what they did the first time around!

Now hear the words of Jesus: "Very truly I tell you, whoever hears my word and believes him who sent me has eternal life and will not be judged but has crossed over from death to life" (John 5:24). Jesus contrasted eternal life with condemnation and death. He was stating categorically that it is possible for us to pass from one to the other and to *know* it! The key to this, He explained, was listening to what He said, understanding who He was, and realizing who had sent Him and therefore on whose behalf He was speaking. In other words, we need to recognize that in Jesus, God the Father was announcing the way to eternal life and not to condemnation. The way was through a glad, wholehearted acceptance of Jesus as the Son of God and a life of trust and obedience to Him based on His claims, His promises, His calling and His purposes.

One more thing: this eternal life of which Jesus spoke was described elsewhere not as something we get when we die but as a *present* experience of knowing God in the here and now that blossoms into fullest reality in eternity. Jesus explained it this way: "This is eternal life: that they know you, the only true God, and Jesus Christ, whom you have sent" (17:3).

This means that once we have made our peace with God and have come into a position of loving, trusting obedience to His Son, Jesus, we have eternal life. Dying is no longer the issue; living the rest of our days on earth in the light of what death leads to is what matters now! "The living should take this to heart" (Eccles. 7:2).

However old we are, we settle down to some basic understandings:

- I know who I am—I'm a sinner saved by grace.
- I know whose I am—I belong to Christ, the Son of God, the risen Lord of life and death. I could not be in better hands.
- I know why I'm still here—I'm here to bring glory to Him through a life of worship and service for as long as He gives me breath.
- I know where I'm going—I'm heading ultimately for the fullness of eternal life, which I have started to taste down here on earth, knowing full well that it will be much better in the new heaven and the new earth!

Now it's all about living well for as much time as we have available. And that should mean considerable improvement. That's solid theology—it's eternal truth!

For Personal Reflection and Group Discussion

Points to Ponder

- Since I brought up shaky theology, let me add a few thoughts on the subject. It seems logical to me that, as everybody knows that life ends in death and that the older we get, the nearer we are to that inevitability, people should give serious consideration to this topic.

- This eternal life of which Jesus spoke was described elsewhere not as something we get when we die but as a *present* experience of knowing God in the here and now that blossoms into fullest reality in eternity.

- I frequently meet people who avoid the subject of the possibility of life beyond the grave at all costs. Others assume that they will go to a better place, but they have no solid ground for their assumptions.

- Jesus contrasted eternal life with condemnation and death with life. He stated categorically that it is possible for us to pass from one to the other and to *know* it!

Discuss/Journal/Pray

1. Spend some time reflecting on the Points to Ponder.
2. What is the key to knowing that we have eternal life?
3. Read John 17:3 and memorize it.
4. However old you are, what are the basic understandings of which you can be certain? What is your theology based on?

A Personal Note from Jill

Can you give a reason that you are sure that you have eternal life? Why don't you share your story with someone?

I came to faith while attending university in the United Kingdom. I was in the hospital at the time, and a nurse explained the good news to me. She offered to pray with me, so I borrowed her words and prayed with her. I prayed simply,

"Lord, I'm sorry. I am a sinner. Thank You for dying on the cross for me. Please come into my heart and transform my life. I want to be Your follower." And He answered my prayer!

You need to make sure that you have given your life to Christ. Would you like to pray now to accept Him by His Spirit into your heart? Prayer is simply talking to God. Just tell Him that you're sorry for your sin and that you need Him to come into your life as Savior and Lord. You won't be sorry!

If you make that decision, be sure that you find a Bible-believing church, pick up an easy-to-understand Bible, and start reading the book of Mark in the New Testament. Keep a prayer journal in which you can write out your prayers to God and make a list of things to pray for. Then tell a friend what has happened to you.

12

THE UPSIDE OF AGING

I hope that you haven't forgotten that the bottom half of the glass is completely full. I guess if we're talking about the aging glass, we need to ask, "Full of what?" Or, if you wish, "What is the upside of the bottom half?"

One thing I love about getting older and coming to terms with it is the new sense of freedom I enjoy. I remember an event that happened shortly before I was due to step aside as senior pastor of the church I had served for thirty years. We routinely held four weekend services—one on Saturday evening and three on Sunday morning. Regularly during the Saturday evening service, I watched carefully for aspects of the service that could be improved, and at the end of the service, our staff would make minor changes for the remaining weekend services. Just a few weeks before I was to resign my position, the church held the final missions-conference weekend of my tenure, during which the missions committee was responsible for all four services. During the Saturday service, I began making mental notes of what we could discuss afterward; but then I thought, *I don't need to do this. This committee does this service once a year! They're doing very well. I'll leave it—and them—alone!*

Then the reality dawned on me: in a few weeks it would be that way all the time! I could relinquish the responsibility for good! As soon as I decided to do so, I sensed the most remarkable feeling of a weight being lifted from my shoulders. The surprising thing, however, is that for the last thirty years, I had never thought a burden was there; I only noticed it after it was gone. I'd had no idea how burdened with responsibility I had been. For thirty years I loved being the senior pastor, but since that time I have equally loved *not* being the senior pastor!

For some women who have devoted themselves to raising a family and supporting their husbands at home, this sense of freedom is not at all welcome and leads to the empty-nest syndrome. Some mothers' sense of worth has been wrapped up in children who are now becoming responsible citizens (hopefully), and they are no longer necessary to the same extent. For her, the need to be needed, which is so much a part of who she is, has suddenly gone, and nothing has taken its place. So what should she do?

For men whose main occupation has taken them outside the home, the situation is somewhat different from that of many women. Such men have been governed by the demands of an increasingly competitive work environment that proved more and more pressurizing by the day. For many of them, their life has become their work, and their work has become their life. Sadly, for many their sense of worth—their identity—has been tied up in their work. And when it is time to lay aside their responsibilities of employment, their sense of self-worth plummets. Huge adjustments await them.

Some embrace their new realities. Looking realistically at themselves, checking on who they are, whose they are, why they're still here and where they're heading, they begin to build the next stage of life. They set about living life focused on certain facts: they were intentionally created by God for His purposes; they have committed their lives to Him and His faithful care; God will reveal to them where a meaningful lifestyle can be developed; and when life is over on earth, they will enter eternity, where life will be lived in all its glorious fullness. In doing this, they find new ways to live responsibly. Having completed one phase of life, they are ready to embrace what lies ahead.

Freedom has two dimensions. Freedom *from*: we no longer have to do what we've been doing for years on end! And freedom *for*: now we have the opportunity to do what we've never done before! This is one of the upsides of aging.

For Personal Reflection and Group Discussion

Points to Ponder

- One thing I love about getting older and coming to terms with it is the new sense of freedom I enjoy.
- For many men, their life has become their work, and their work has become their life.
- Some embrace their new realities. Looking realistically at themselves, they find new ways to live responsibly. Having completed one phase of life, they are ready to embrace what lies ahead.
- Freedom has two dimensions. Freedom *from*: we no longer have to do what we've been doing for years on

end! And freedom *for*: now we have the opportunity to do what we've never done before! This is one of the upsides of aging.

Discuss/Journal/Pray

1. Spend some time reflecting on the Points to Ponder.
2. Do you feel more irrelevant as you get older, as if you are not needed?
3. Do you feel positive about the freedom that aging offers you, or do you struggle to adapt to it?
4. Share ideas about some of the upsides that this new phase of life can bring.

A Personal Note from Jill

The famous author James Michener used to tell a story about a neighbor—a farmer who had an old apple tree that had ceased to bear fruit. The farmer hammered eight nails into the unproductive fruit tree, resulting in a bumper crop. The farmer's explanation was that the rusty nails hammered into its trunk shocked the tree into remembering that its job was to produce apples. This story reminded me of Psalm 92:14, "Even in old age they will still produce fruit; they will remain vital and green" (NLT), and it inspired me to write the following poem:

> The greenness of gray in life's later stage,
> The freshness of soul that refuses to age,
> Is grown in the garden of God in my heart;
> It's the fruit of the Spirit as God does His part.

The greenness of gray—a freshness of mind
That proclaims His great power and love for man-
kind,
A love for the children who don't know His grace
Gives purpose and reason to finish my race.

Pray this prayer: "You promised me, Lord, that if I'm planted in Your garden of grace, the world around me will see the greenness in my life and ministry and be refreshed by the fruit of Your Spirit."[1]

13

FREE TO BE RESPONSIBLE

George Washington, in his farewell address in 1796, said, "Every day the increasing weight of years admonishes me more and more that the shade of retirement is as necessary to me as it will be welcome."[1]

Washington was only in his early fifties when he began to feel "the increasing weight of years," which speaks both to the relatively short lifespan of American men in the eighteenth century and also to the intense pressure and hardship that he endured in his two terms as president of the United States. Duly admonished, he turned his thoughts longingly to the "shade of retirement," finding those thoughts both necessary and welcome!

No doubt, many twenty-first century American men would echo the same sentiments if not the identical vocabulary. For them, the thought of not having to work anymore, of freedom, of responsibilities laid down has obvious appeal. That's why they can't wait to retire. When I began my career in banking as a seventeen-year-old, I was told by a wonderful man who took me under his wing, "The bank won't pay you much for some time, but they guarantee a good pension, so you can look forward to a comfortable retirement." At seventeen I was somewhat taken aback by this and wondered where he was going with this information. I didn't have to wait, for he added, "Do you see those men working the tills on the counter? All of them are just putting in time until retirement, and they've been doing it for years! You can do better than that. Don't buy into that philosophy." I was shocked—but not as shocked as I subsequently was to find that this attitude of just putting in time isn't foreign to the pastorate either!

Some people want to play for the majority of their retirement days. Work is over, so they welcome playtime! This is the same mentality that inspired the well-known restaurant TGI Friday's. In case you're not aware, TGIF purports to praise the Lord for inventing workless weekends—presumably because work is onerous. This upsets some churchgoers, whom I've heard say, "The Bible doesn't mention retirement." To that it must be admitted that the Bible says nothing about computers, flush toilets or sliced bread either, but they are all facts of modern life—as is retirement.

What then is retirement all about? What is its purpose for the Christian? We were created to work—that's what human beings do! God worked, God put man to work, Jesus worked, the apostles worked and the Scriptures have plenty to say on the subject for our benefit. Granted, the Fall, which messed everything up, messed up work, which meant that work can and probably does sometimes become onerous, sweaty and boring, but we're called to do it anyway. We're to remember, of course, that redemption rolls back the Fall's consequences, including the downside of labor. Redemption can easily transform work. Or, perhaps more accurately, redemption transforms workers' attitudes to life in general and to work in particular. We therefore need a theology of work, among other things. Retirement—which has been for many men the pot of gold at the end of the rainbow—cannot simply be a matter of not having to work anymore.

Retirement does not mean quitting working; it means staying busy being productive, despite no longer being employed! Retirement may involve not having a boss, not having to meet quotas, not having to satisfy customers or shareholders or boards or government regulations, and not having to do stuff we don't want to do anymore or never wanted to do. It means we have the freedom to do things we've always wanted to do and the chance to discover new things we never previously considered.

It is important to remember that even though George Washington was eager to exchange the pressures and challenges of life on the frontlines for the tranquility of his beloved home, Mount Vernon, he did not go home to lie in a hammock. He set about dealing with a problem that had become more apparent to him during his years serving his country: the issue of slavery. He made arrangements for the emancipation of his slaves and for the care of his wife, put his affairs in order and died two years later. He was productive until the end.

Just in case you're wondering, I'm not opposed to playing or relaxing or resting or taking it easy! While God worked and put the human race to work, He also took a day off and ordained that human beings should do the same. In our modern era, in which machines do a lot of our work for us, we can take a little more time off than in days gone by. Retirement done properly involves meaningful, productive labor, lots of down time, and the responsible use of newfound freedoms!

In his wonderful book *Man's Search for Meaning*, Viktor E. Frankl wrote, "The Statue of Liberty on the East Coast should be supplemented by a Statue of Responsibility on the West Coast."[2] In other words, every time we see the Statue of Liberty, we should consider a responsible use of freedom—particularly if we're retired.

For Personal Reflection and Group Discussion

Points to Ponder

- There's a big difference between not working and not being employed.
- We were created to work.
- We need a theology of work, among other things.
- Retirement does not mean quitting working; it means staying busy being productive, despite no longer being employed!
- Every time you see the Statue of Liberty, consider a responsible use of freedom.

Discuss/Journal/Pray

1. Spend some time reflecting on the Points to Ponder.
2. How do I avoid allowing work to become my life?
3. What can I do to start formulating a theology of work?

4. What is the difference between not working and not being employed?
5. What does God want me to do with the freedom of retirement?

A Personal Note from Jill

My friend Arn Quakelaar retired early from his career as an executive with an international corporation because he had a desire to address the pressing needs he had seen on his way to work each day in Milwaukee's inner city. He formed a ministry called BASICS, which stands for "Brothers and Sisters in Christ Serving." It is a ministry that informs and enthuses, motivates and mobilizes, as Arn's team moves into every echelon of the city's life, bringing encouragement and help and leaving a trail of blessing.

What are some dreams you've always had, or what excites you about this season of your life? Dare to be an Arn, and see what doors God might open. Remember, retirement means staying busy being productive.

14

TAKING IT EASY

I think leisure is a first cousin of freedom. The responsible use of freedom for older people means continuing to do things of value, and it also means not continuing to do the same volume of things we did before with the same intensity and the same obligations. But what do we do with the time that is no longer consumed by all the things we once did? And what do we do with the energy no longer being expended on these former things?

As far as energy is concerned, you may have noticed that yours is not as abundant as it was in former days! If that is not the case right now, be patient—it will be sooner or later. Having a surplus of energy is a rapidly diminishing issue. You will, however, have the same amount of time each day that you've always had, so there can easily be a surplus of hours after all the things that have to be done are done. What should we do with them? Some would say, "Do nothing!" But that gets old in a hurry. As we sit around, the body deteriorates more rapidly, the brain atrophies, friendships wither, boredom increases and feelings of meaninglessness multiply. We were made for something much better than doing nothing!

After having effective pastoral ministries in various positions, a good friend of mine decided in his advancing years to focus on seniors, his contemporaries. He and his wife moved into a trailer park and immediately discovered a lot of people with nowhere to go, nothing to do and no one to do it with—and that was about it! Aging for these individuals meant sitting around waiting for something to happen. Rarely did anything happen, and when something did, it was rarely good.

Another friend made a similar move after having ministered in more traditional roles for many years. He and his wife also moved to a trailer park. Their experience was much different. Big time! The park covered many beautiful groomed acres in the sunbelt and accommodated hundreds of luxurious trailers. My understanding of trailer parks required an immediate revision. Their trailer was luxury on wheels! Most of the owners of these comfortable homes had beautiful houses up north and were quintessential snowbirds. They had lots of leisure time; but unlike the people in the trailers on the other side of the tracks, their leisure time was full—although mainly full of fun and games.

Six or seven years ago, my wife met a gentleman during the coffee hour between services at our home church. He told her that he was paying his first visit to the church and that the purpose of his visit was to meet someone he referred to as his pastor. When my wife inquired as to who his pastor was, she was surprised to hear that I was the person he had in mind. In some way, apparently, I was pastoring a man I'd never met. Further inquiries revealed that this man, who became a firm friend, owned a condominium on the Mexican Riviera. For a number of years, he had been gathering videotapes of my messages and playing them on a TV set in the restaurant bar of the complex where he and hundreds of other northerners spent the winter months. Without knowing it, we had planted a church in Mexico!

We were invited to travel down to meet our "congregation." We ended up repeating the visit three or four times each year. The last time we visited, we noted that remarkable things were happening through this group of North Americans. They had taken seriously the messages we had preached and had intentionally moved out into the towns and barrios near their complex. There they had started work among prisoners and drug addicts, established trade schools, opened a Christian coffee bar on the main street of the nearest downtown, and assisted local churches however they could serve them. In case you're wondering, however, they still had time for swimming, dining, golfing and bird-watching. Leisure time is another upside of aging, but it is to be invested, not spent! Enjoying leisure is not doing nothing; it means exerting less energy and taking more time doing it. It means taking it easy!

One day when I was on a run—part of a regular exercise regimen that I had practiced for many years—I started to ask myself questions: "How long have I been doing this? How many miles have I run? Is this activity slightly ridiculous for a man of my age? Is it possible that some people will feel sorry for me and rush to help me because they think I'm stumbling? Why am I still doing this?" I found no answers for the questions except for the one about people confusing my running with stumbling. I thought further about this situation and concluded that as I was tired, hot and sticky, the only thing fast about my running was the speed at which my times were nose-diving. So I walked home! This was another liberating moment, not dissimilar to the one I experienced just before I stepped aside as senior pastor—a sense of relief, a relaxation of tension and an immediate introduction to new horizons. Well, not horizons, actually, because my new discoveries were right in front of me. As I walked home that day, instead of being focused on beating my previous time with regular glances at my stopwatch, I instead wiped the sweat from my eyes and noticed the flowers in the hedgerow. Then I heard the song of the birds. With great joy, I slowly inhaled the warm fresh air of the countryside through which I had pounded hundreds of times. A couple of times, I paused to more closely inspect tiny blossoms that had no doubt been there for some time but that I had never noticed before. I walked slowly. When I got home, my wife asked me, "What happened to you?"

A disclaimer at this point: This is not a diatribe against vigorous exercise, which I happen to believe has contributed to my longevity. I have simply exchanged running for walking. I have traded beating my own times for focusing on God's handiwork and have swapped panting laboriously for inhaling slowly. I'm taking things a little easier! There are a thousand ways this can be applied. It's an upside to aging—it's called being more leisurely about living.

For Personal Reflection and Group Discussion

Points to Ponder

- I think leisure is the first cousin of freedom. The responsible use of freedom for older people means continuing to do things of value, and it also means not continuing to do the same volume of things we did before with the same intensity and the same obligations. But what do we do with the time that is no longer consumed by all the things we once did?
- Leisure time is another upside of aging, but it has to be invested, not spent!
- Leisure is not doing nothing.

Discuss/Journal/Pray

1. Spend some time reflecting on the Points to Ponder.
2. What does "taking it easy" mean to you?
3. How do you invest your leisure time?
4. Do you feel guilty for not doing "good works" in your leisure time?
5. Stay quiet and share your feelings with God.

A Personal Note from Jill

Read the first two chapters of Genesis.

1. What did God do with:
   - His work time? And what did He think about the work He had done?
   - His leisure time?

2. What did Adam and Eve do with:
   - Their work time?
   - Their leisure time?

3. Read Genesis 3. The Fall affected both work and leisure. How does this chapter reveal its effects?

4. Read Genesis 3:15 again. Note that God did not curse the woman or the man.
   - Whom and what did He curse?
   - What did God promise?

5. Read John 3:16 and Hebrews 2:14–15.
   - What is the connection between these verses and the promise of Genesis 3:15?
   - Pray about this.
   - Ask God if He wants you to change one thing in your leisure time. Make a plan to do what He shows you.

15

PRODUCTIVE LEISURE

I suspect my use of the term "responsible freedom" may sound vaguely oxymoronic to some people. Here's another one for consideration: how about "productive leisure?" Productive leisure is the opposite of doing nothing.

I have heard from not a few wives on their recently retired husbands, "They just sit around the place getting under my feet, and I wish they'd find something to do." Finding something to do would probably be a good idea in such circumstances, both as a means of easing the wife's blood pressure and saving the husband from the wife's sharp tongue, for which he recently unknowingly traded the eagle eye of his boss. But productive leisure involves more than just finding something to do.

We all know that Genesis talks about God creating the world in six days and then taking the seventh day off. We've also no doubt heard about the rhythms of work and leisure that the normal workweek is designed to protect. This is not to say that all societies are equally committed to that principle or that many people who profess to be committed to it actually live by it; but ideally, at least, we understand that there is a time for work and rest, for activity and the cessation of activity. No mandate exists for human beings to completely stop all intentional activity—activity that produces something of value. When this kind of activity is continued in later life, in which more free time is available, I call it productive leisure.

An old farmer in the north of England (where I grew up) employed and housed a young farmhand. He told me that one day he asked the young man, "John, what do you do in your free time?" John thought for a moment and then said, "Sometimes I sits and thinks, but most times I just sits." Knowing how hard some of those young farmhands worked, I am not surprised that at times he did nothing at all. His body was exhausted, and he needed rest—recuperative, healing rest—to fit him for the next day's labor. What is troubling about the young man's answer, however, is that while sometimes he used his leisure productively—he spent time in thought—most times he just sat! That is unproductive leisure, and it is what upsets wives of recently retired men—and sometimes old farmers. It is not the ideal for which we were created.

Leisure affords physical rest and recuperation as well as the opportunity for reflective thought and meditation. We are not told what God did on His day off, but we do know that He delighted in what He had made. He studied His creation, thought about it, evaluated it and was pleased with the results. He ceased from His work, but He still did something: "God saw all that he had made, and it was very good" (Gen. 1:31). God created time, space and matter out of nothing and then transformed matter into a myriad of different forms—all of which were incredibly intricate, orderly, beautiful and purposeful—and He delighted in them! He placed humans, created in His own image and filled with His own life-giving force, in charge. I wonder if God just *sat* and rejoiced in all that filled His vision and *thought* about all that was involved. We do know that He took cool evening walks in the garden and expected Adam and Eve to join Him. Did they walk in silence; or did they commune together, enjoying each other and sharing excitement about the wonders of creation?

Here's another upside of aging: we can actually have the time to sit, rest, think, meditate and go for walks! This is particularly valuable if life, up until aging kicked in, had been a frantic, frenetic round of things to do that never ended and pressures that never eased. Instead of living a harried, tense, there-aren't-enough-hours-in-the-day lifestyle, a more ordered approach of seeking to spend time well becomes the order of the day. Life used to be a matter of "What do I have to do next?" and "What did I forget to do that can't wait?" Now we can think about new things, great things, fascinating things—things we never knew existed, and things we wish we'd always known.

Perhaps a good topic of reflection is, "What do I do with my leisure time in a leisurely fashion, free from the demands under which I formerly worked, that will allow me time and opportunity to explore life in a way I never before considered? What books need to be read, what topics need to be learned, what skills could be developed, what service could I offer, what needs should I meet, which people should I seek to know—all of which would yield a productive use of my leisure time?"

For Personal Reflection and Group Discussion

Points to Ponder

- Productive leisure involves more than finding something to do.
- Leisure affords physical rest and recuperation as well as the opportunity for reflective thought and meditation.
- Here's another upside of aging: you actually have time to sit, rest, think and meditate.
- Instead of living a harried, tense, there-aren't-enough-hours-in-the-day lifestyle, a more ordered approach of seeking to spend time well becomes the order of the day. It used to be a matter of "What do I have to do next?" and "What did I forget to do that can't wait?" Now we can think about new things, great things, fascinating things—things we never knew existed and things we wish we'd always known.

Discuss/Journal/Pray

1. Spend some time reflecting on the Points to Ponder.
2. How can you be more productive in your leisure time?
3. In thinking about all the new things, great things and fascinating things that you could do, answer the following questions:
   - What books need to be read?
   - What subjects need to be learned?
   - What skills could be developed?

- What services could be offered?
- What needs should I meet?
- Which people should I get to know?

(Please don't attempt all of these at once, though, or you will have no leisure time left! Start with one.)

A Personal Note from Jill

Stuart and I are very different (opposites attract remember?), so we find renewal in different ways. When we go for a walk, he likes to stretch his legs, while I like to stop and chat with every stranger, kiss every baby and pet every dog. He watches movies that challenge his thinking; I want only happy endings. We have to give each other space to relax in our different ways.

It stresses me out to stop doing physical things. But if instead of trying to stop completely, I simply change my activity and do something different from my daily responsibilities, my body, mind and soul are renewed. For example, if I garden or do something artsy like write a poem, I find refreshment. Remember the old adage, "A change is as good as a rest."

How do you best replenish?

16

THE JOY OF READING

James Boswell wrote in *The Life of Samuel Johnson*, "A man ought to read just as inclination leads him; for what he reads as a task will do him little good."[1] I'm sure that businessmen who read reports and attorneys who read briefs would not agree that the things they had to read did them "little good," but Boswell has a point. Reading leisurely because we want to do it and have time to do it is entirely different from reading articles that we have to understand for an important meeting or memorizing manuals or even following recipes to cook meals.

In high school I was required to read Shakespeare. I'm afraid William the Bard did little for me at the time; but in my advanced years, I have returned to my old friend and found his use of language refreshing and invigorating and his writing a thing of beauty, wisdom and remarkable insight.

Where then does an inclination to read come into the equation? One of my adult grandsons recently remarked on the fact that, as he put it, "Poppa spends a lot of time reading." The note of wonder in his voice hinted at the fact that he found this to be at least slightly strange. "Why do you do it?" he asked me. "Michael," I told him, "the older I get, the more I realize how much I don't know. But more than that, as I recognize not only that my ignorance is monumental, I know that my opportunities to do something about it are rapidly disappearing. In other words, I'm running out of time." I've always *had* to read to a large extent; but now I have the inclination to read in my leisure time, because the more I thoughtfully ponder the world God has created and the people He has placed in it, the more fascinated I am by His handiwork. I am also the more alerted to and appalled by the depth of our fallenness, and I am more thrilled by every piece of evidence of God's redemptive interventions. I want to know more. And so I read to learn, because my curiosity has been married to my lack of knowledge and a sense of urgency. These in turn have been channeled into my leisure time and invested in the most richly available resource imaginable: books. That's where my inclination comes from—in abundance. So I'm a reader.

Paul Tournier, the Swiss doctor, said that reading is "a window on the world, on its extreme diversity and its inexhaustible riches," and he called "a good book . . . a wonderful treasure of quiet enjoyment."[2] Of course it is! When we read a classic novel, we are introduced to another person's understanding of the world in which we live and the behaviors of the people with whom we share this world. Reading Victor Hugo's *Les Miserables* opened my eyes. Digging into Charles Dickens' *A Tale of Two Cities* touched me deeply. And at the risk of being accused of joking, let me recommend *The Guernsey Literary and Potato Peel Pie Society* by Mary Ann Shaffer and Annie Barrows. It's not yet a classic, but it may be on its way to such elevated status despite, or perhaps because of, its title.

If we read history, we can discern the patterns and developments, the mistakes and divine interventions, of years gone by. Perhaps we can even see visions of the future. Shakespeare said it best:

> There is a history in all men's lives,
> Figuring the nature of the times deceased,
> The which observed, a man may prophecy,
> With a near aim, of the main chance of things
> As yet not come to life, which in their seeds
> And weak beginnings lie intreasured.[3]

Of course he could simply have said, "History repeats itself," but where would the literary appeal have been in that?! If it's World War II you want to learn about, read B.H. Liddell Hart's *History of the Second World War*. If you prefer the American Civil War, Jeff Shaara's *Gods and Generals* is a great read.

By delving into biography, we learn about the circumstances of someone's early days, which fashioned their latter years. We recognize in others the tendencies that have dogged our own lives. You might start with Eric Metaxas' *Bonhoeffer: Pastor, Martyr, Prophet, Spy* or Alister McGrath's *C.S. Lewis—A Life* or H.W. Brands' fascinating story about Benjamin Franklin titled *The First American*. Of course, since I am a Brit, anything about Churchill catches my attention!

Theology, naturally, also interests me greatly—Gordon D. Fee's *God's Empowering Presence* taught me much. Christopher J.H. Wright's *The Mission of God* broadened my vision. John R.W. Stott's *The Cross of Christ* is, in my opinion, without parallel.

Mark Twain was perhaps a little over the top when he wrote, "The man who does not read has no advantage over the man who cannot read";[4] but he had a point worth considering, particularly if we have some free time and have not gotten around to using it productively. Find a quiet corner and a comfortable chair, play some soft background music and settle down with a good book. You won't be under your wife's feet, you won't be told to find something to do, your world will be enlarged, and you'll find some new topics to share and discuss with your friends and family.

For Personal Reflection and Group Discussion

Points to Ponder

- "A man ought to read just as inclination leads him; for what he reads as a task will do him little good" (James Boswell).
- The older I get, the more I realize how much I don't know, and I'm running out of time.
- Reading is "a kind of initiation into new aspects of life" (Paul Tournier).
- Find a quiet corner and a comfortable chair, play some soft background music and settle down with a good book.

Discuss/Journal/Pray

1. Spend some time reflecting on the Points to Ponder.
2. Talk with friends about the books you are reading, and invite suggestions for new books from them.

3. Develop your own system of marking, highlighting and note-taking. This helps to more deeply impress upon your mind what you have read and helps preserve important thoughts that might otherwise escape your memory.

A Personal Note from Jill

Here's an idea: start a book club. Invite a few friends to make suggestions of books that may be of general interest. Pick one, and work out a reading schedule. Don't make it too onerous! Then agree when and how often to meet in order to share what you learn, what you find interesting and what you do not agree with. The fellowship that develops and the mutual edification that results will more than repay the time and effort invested in the venture. Read a variety of books so that everyone in your group stretches their minds and hearts together.

17

THE BEST BOOK

I talked a couple of chapters back about meditation and would like to return briefly to this topic, because I want to be clear about what I mean—and do not mean—by meditating. With the relatively recent advent of Eastern mysticism and oriental practices in the West, we have seen a burgeoning interest in meditative techniques. Perhaps this is an effort to alleviate the Western penchant for high blood pressure and other stress-induced ailments.

These techniques, which vary widely, all have their roots in Hinduism. Some saw numerous migrations and reincarnations before arriving at their present commercialized Western forms, while others are still strongly influenced by Hindu belief systems. All of them, however, differ dramatically from Christian meditation. All forms of Eastern meditation focus on emptying the mind of thoughts of earth, while Christian meditation focuses on filling the mind with thoughts of God.

The prerequisite for Christian meditation is the reading of Scripture, upon which the mind will then be concentrated. This will lead readers and meditators to think deeply and prayerfully about God's Word—the best book we can read in our leisure time. It will encourage them to look to the Holy

Spirit to engage them in the deep recesses of their souls in order to bring fresh enlightenment, encouragement, insight, instruction and understanding.

The psalmist describes the man who is truly blessed, and there is no doubt in his mind that one of the reasons for his blessed experience is that "his delight is in the law of the LORD, and on his law he meditates day and night" (Ps. 1:2, ESV). Years later Paul said to Timothy, his young associate and friend, "Reflect on what I am saying, for the Lord will give you insight into all this" (2 Tim. 2:7). So the intent is clear. Reading or listening to the Scripture requires careful, thoughtful contemplation to have a proper understanding of what the Word is saying.

Many people tell me that their lives are so busy that they don't have time to read and meditate on Scripture. For many of them, their weekly intake of biblical truth is limited to one sermon lasting anywhere from twenty to forty-five minutes maximum. Many of those listening to a sermon don't carry a Bible to which they can refer for clarification. Many more don't take notes on what is said for careful reference, so the chances of thoughtful, subsequent meditation on the Word preached are understandably slim. This is far from being a spiritually healthy situation, but at least more leisure time in aging gives us a wonderful opportunity to make up for some lost time.

During World War II, Dietrich Bonhoeffer founded a seminary under the noses of the Nazis, at some considerable risk, in Finkenwalde, Germany. It is interesting to note that in such tense circumstances, he required all students to spend a half hour every day meditating on Scripture. This was, of course, in addition to the intense study of biblical theology, and it is important to recognize the differentiation he made between studying God's Word and meditating upon it. "Just as you do not analyze the words of someone you love, but accept them as they are said to you, accept the Word of Scripture and ponder it in your heart, as Mary did. That is all. That is meditation."[1]

Bonhoeffer, a confirmed bachelor at age thirty-six, surprised everybody by falling in love with a beautiful young woman called Maria who was much younger than himself. Maria's father and brother were both killed on the Russian front. Her mother was understandably deeply distressed, and she felt emotionally incapable of dealing with her young daughter's possible love affair with a much older man, so she asked Dietrich and Maria not to meet. This they agreed to, but a correspondence flourished between them. To read their letters, included in Bonhoeffer's biography,[2] is to see into the hearts of people writing and reading out of love. It was in this fashion that Bonhoeffer encouraged his students to approach Scripture—with delight and anticipation.

We should also use our "sanctified imagination" when reading Scripture, especially the narrative passages in which real people lived and moved in real situations. We imagine ourselves standing in their sandals and hear God's words to our own hearts—pondering our understanding of them, gauging our reactions to them, living in the joy of them, facing the challenge of them. This is meditating, and it enriches the soul and draws us into deeper fellowship with the Lord we love. And at last we have time to do it!

We could start with meditating on Psalm 119—the longest chapter in the Bible, in which practically every verse refers to the Scriptures. The psalmist uses different words for the Scriptures and for his approach to them. For instance, he talks about statutes, precepts, ordinances, promises, decrees and commands (all these terms require meditating upon!). He also testifies, "I seek you with all my heart," "I have hidden your word in my heart," "I rejoice in following your statutes," "I meditate on your precepts," "I delight in your decrees," "I will not neglect your word" (see Ps. 119:9–16). In this psalm we note the psalmist's "inclination," to use James Boswell's term. He wants to know how he can "stay on the path of purity" and how to be "living according to [God's] word." He says, "I seek you with all my heart," and he fears to "stray from [God's] commands." He does not want to "sin against" God; he says, "I rejoice," concerning what he is learning, and, "I delight," regarding discovering the decrees of the Lord. That's why he reads, listens to and meditates regularly and joyfully on God's Word.

Those of us who live in the West, unlike many of our brothers and sisters in other parts of the world, are richly endowed with spiritual resources. In addition to Bibles in a variety of translations, we have devotionals for personal study, books on every imaginable subject, classes of every kind, churches on every street corner and in every suburb, radio preachers, TV preachers, the Internet, blogs, MP3s, and so on, *ad infinitum*. And now we have the time to avail ourselves of those opportunities.

A word of caution may not be out of place here: With the plethora of material and the ready access that we all have to communication-delivery systems, much of the material available is trivial at best and downright dangerous at worst. Discernment is vitally necessary. Ask yourself some serious questions: "Does this ministry honor Christ? Is it solidly based on the exposition of Scripture? Or is it simply telling me what I know, reiterating what I want to hear? Is it stretching my mind, challenging my presuppositions, broadening my vision, taking me deeper into Christ, and requiring me to search the Word more carefully?" You could say, "Is it helping me improve with age?"

For Personal Reflection and Group Discussion

Points to Ponder

- The prerequisite of Christian meditation is the reading of Scripture, upon which the mind will then be concentrated. Paul said succinctly to Timothy, his young associate and friend, "Reflect on what I am saying, for the Lord will give you insight into all this" (2 Tim. 2:7).
- Reading or listening to Scripture requires careful, thoughtful contemplation to have proper understanding of what the Word is saying.
- For many, a weekly intake of biblical truth is limited to one sermon lasting anywhere from twenty to forty-five minutes. This is far from being a spiritually healthy situation, but more leisure time in aging gives us a wonderful opportunity to make up for some lost time.

- We should use our "sanctified imagination" when reading Scripture.

Discuss/Journal/Pray

1. Spend some time reflecting on the Points to Ponder.
2. We are often asked, "Why are there so many translations of the Bible?" The Bible was not written in English, so careful translation from one language to another was needed. But our knowledge of other languages is growing daily, so our translations can be more accurate as time passes. Second, our language is not static. New words appear, and older words disappear, so a good translation needs to be understandable to modern people.
3. Which translation of the Bible do you find most helpful? Why?
4. Are you reading the Word in healthy amounts? If not, what can you do to make up for lost time?
5. What opportunities can you take advantage of to increase your love, understanding and knowledge of the Word?

A Personal Note from Jill

As a new believer, I was met with a barrage of opinions about the Bible—dogmatic statements and strange ideas! I was a university student and was bewildered about the conflicting views to which I was being introduced. I longed to be sure that what I was learning to believe was actually true. As time went by, Psalm 119:18 became both a source of comfort and a prayer. I use it to this day: "Open my eyes that I may see wonderful things in your law." As time has gone on, I began to say, "Your servant will meditate on your decrees. Your statutes are my delight; they are my counselors" (119:23–24).

Read and meditate on Psalm 119:33–40.

18

IT TAKES TWO TO COMMUNICATE

C ommunication is not easy. When I was a senior pastor, our staff occasionally surveyed our congregation to solicit people's suggestions, complaints and other feedback. One regular complaint was that the church did not communicate information clearly, so we tried different ways to effectively communicate.

I noticed, however, that it didn't matter if we printed our announcements, announced them verbally, displayed them on the screen, enacted them in a drama or, in more recent times, put everything on a website—some people still phoned the office and asked for details that had been carefully communicated! The problem was that printing information required people to read, announcing it required listening, projecting or enacting it necessitated people paying attention and, to the consternation of many old timers, the website required logging on. In other words, communication has to be a two-way street.

In the unique conversation that is the privilege of every child of God, God speaks to mankind, and mankind carefully listens and then responds. God speaks to us through His Word—the Scriptures—which we older people have the time and desire to dig into. We have learned that we need to listen, but responding is also required. Our response is called worship, which includes prayer. Bible reading and prayer are two sides of the same street.

I have found in my efforts to communicate with my adult grandchildren that they rarely answer their phones and never seem to check their e-mail. If I leave a phone message for them to "please return my call," it rarely happens! Fortunately, if I text them, it works like a dream—they will respond in seconds, even if they're in class! Prayerlessness is failure to return God's call. Not returning calls is discourteous!

Paul is a great example of what I'm talking about. Have you ever noticed how frequently in his epistles he outlines some great spiritual truth and then pauses to pray about it? You will find him both praising God and interceding for others so that they might discover and experience what God is revealing through him.

Prayer is much more than bringing our petitions to God. To expand on what it means to pray, I will use the acrostic PRAY.

P—Praise

Reading and meditating on God's Word touches our heart and enriches our mind; seeing His handiwork in creation delights our soul. As a result, praise articulates our joy and gratitude. Giving thanks at mealtimes maintains a rhythm of praise, and singing and humming praise songs fosters an attitude of praise. I know a widow lady who is now in her nineties, still living alone, and who can often be heard singing her favorite hymns—she's working her way through her favorite hymnbook. And I love the story of the little Dutch boy standing gazing at the beauty of the tulip fields in full bloom. "Well done, God," he said to no one in particular, except to the Father. Praise!

R—Repentance

Focusing on God's grace, love and kindness almost inevitably highlights, by stark contrast, how ungodly we are, so we bow in repentance and confession. The longer we sit in the sun, the more obvious our wrinkles become; the closer we stand to the mirror, the more clearly we see our flaws. In the modern world, we know so much psychology that our spiritual flaws and wrinkles are frequently described in learned terms and are treated with sophisticated therapies so we can easily forget that sin still exists, that repentance is a necessity and that forgiveness is freely offered. John the aged apostle wrote, "If we claim to be without sin, we deceive ourselves and the truth is not in us. If we confess our sins, he is faithful and just and will forgive us our sins and purify us from all unrighteousness" (1 John 1:8–9). There's no other way to respond to this principle but in prayer.

A—Asking

It's natural for us to be primarily interested in ourselves, but praise and repentance rectify that somewhat, as they help us learn to focus on others. Thus we ask, or intercede, for others to experience what we are learning to desire for ourselves. It is also helpful for us to bear in mind that when Jesus taught His disciples to pray, He encouraged them to ask for daily bread, spiritual guidance, protection and forgiveness. But first they were to outline three major concerns: that God's name would be honored, that His will would be done on earth and that His kingdom would come. Doing this helps us keep our asking in perspective—our needs are not insignificant, but neither are they all-important.

𝒴—Yourself

Practicing the first three dimensions of prayer puts us in a place in which our own desires and aspirations are more closely aligned to what God has in mind for us. With self in its proper place, we are less likely to "ask amiss" (James 4:3, KJV).

I cringe when I hear some older believers tell me they feel as if they no longer have a place in the life of the church. I cringe even more when I hear them say, "I suppose the only thing I can do now is pray," as if prayer is the last resort for sidelined people whose practical usefulness has seen better days. The reality is that many of us can dramatically improve in our aging if only through the discovery that, having been too busy to pray more than perfunctory prayers for years, we are now freed up to discover the joys of communion with the Lord. Effective prayer is powerful. The greatly enlarging thought, as my wife Jill likes to say, is that we can go anywhere in the world on our knees.

Lord, teach us to pray!

For Personal Reflection and Group Discussion

Points to Ponder

- In the unique conversation that is the privilege of every child of God, God speaks to mankind, and mankind carefully listens and then responds.
- Bible reading and prayer are two sides of the same street.
- Prayerlessness is failure to return God's call. Not returning calls is discourteous!
- We can go anywhere in the world on our knees.

Discuss/Journal/Pray

1. Spend some time reflecting on the Points to Ponder.
2. Check out the acrostic PRAY and use it as a pattern for your own prayer life.
3. In which area of prayer from the acrostic are you the weakest? Try journaling this week about that area, and commit to spending more time in prayer focusing on that.
4. Where in the world is God asking you to go on your knees? For whom?

A Personal Note from Jill

When we were teaching our small children to pray at bedtime, we simplified matters by showing them how to pray "please prayers," "thank-you prayers" and "sorry prayers." On one occasion my husband was praying with our eldest child, David. He was full of please prayers, so he needed reminders for thank-you prayers, and he couldn't think of any sorry prayers. Only after something of a standoff did he eventually pray, "Dear Lord, I am so very, very, very sorry that my sister has been such a little snot today!"

Which aspect of prayer is most difficult for you? Why not pray about that?

19

THE NEXT GENERATION—AND THE NEXT

On the occasion of Jill's and my fiftieth wedding anniversary, we managed, after a lot of work, to gather our three children, their spouses, and eleven of our thirteen grandchildren in the same place at the same time. (One grandson was working, and another was in the military, so unfortunately neither of them could join us.) As I looked around the assembled group, I realized that fifty years previous, only Jill and I had existed! We were responsible, in some measure, for the rest of their (except the three in-laws) lives. I thought that we perhaps deserved a little credit for them being alive— and undoubtedly we bore a lot of responsibility.

Parental responsibility is clearly defined when children are dependent. It becomes something of a challenge, however, when they approach adolescence, and it is an entirely different proposition when they become adults. Many parents seem to think that their parental obligations end when a child reaches eighteen; but no matter how old a child may be, parents are still parents for a lifetime.

A whole new era dawns when our adult children have children of their own and we, the aging ones, are anointed "Grandma" and "Grandpa" or, in our case, "Nana Jill" and "Poppa Stu." When grandchildren are young and grandparents don't look old enough to have reached their mature status, grandparenting is new and exciting and relatively easy. Grandparents can pick up the kids whenever they wish and can return them to their parents when they've had them long enough. You've no doubt heard a wise-cracking Grandpa say, "Grandparenting is so much fun that if we'd known it, we'd have had grandkids first," or, "Grandkids are God's reward for raising kids."

When grandchildren become young adults, the situation changes. The relationship is still capable of producing a lot of fun, but it can also bring its share of heartaches, concerns and disappointments. Grandparents don't have the same amount of energy they previously had, and they're more set in their ways than they were in the past. At the same time, grandchildren are more independent, busier, and possibly further away from grandparental thinking than ever before. Grandparents may now have to stand in line behind girl-friends and boyfriends, coaches and bosses, sports and jobs in order to get near their grandkids. Sometimes when I'm asked by friends with young grandchildren if we enjoy having our grandchildren over, I reply, tongue firmly in cheek, "We enjoy it immensely whenever they can fit us into their busy schedules." But regardless of their grandchildren's ages, grandparents still have a role to fulfill in the lives of their grandchildren.

THE NEXT GENERATION—AND THE NEXT

With more women choosing or needing to work outside the home in addition to raising their families, it is not uncommon now for grandparents to undertake a major role in their grandchildren's upbringing. This is even more pronounced when, for instance, families break up and newly divorced, single parents return to their family home out of necessity, or when young people experience difficulty in finding a job that provides a living wage and choose to live with their grandparents. I have great sympathy for many young people today who have diligently continued their studies, graduated from college, and now hold a diploma in one hand and a huge bill for school fees in the other but can find no suitable job that matches their qualifications. They need help, and grandparents are often the ones in the best place to offer it.

We have had the pleasure and challenge of having one of our twentysomething grandsons live with us for four years. We have greatly enjoyed having him around the place; he has risen early on frequent occasions to drive us to the airport and has picked us up again late at night. He has provided company for Jill when I have traveled. At the same time, he has turned one of our neat bedrooms into a disaster area, turned night into day with a sleep disorder that he developed in college, and delighted in practicing culinary experiments that have filled the air with mysterious smells and the fridge with strange leftovers! When he chose to move on, he told us of his decision to "leave home" with teary eyes, and we were sad to see him go. We knew, however, that he was moving on in far better shape than when he had arrived four years prior. That's grandparenting in the modern era.

I have recently embarked on an experiment. It's an attempt to encourage my grandchildren to deepen their relationships with each other. We have thirteen of them—one in Florida, two in Minneapolis, one in Atlanta, three in Chicago, one in Abilene, one in Austin, one in Dallas and three in the Milwaukee area, where Jill and I live. I told them all that I wanted news from each one of them every month that I would collate, comment on and distribute—a kind of cousins' newsletter. Most of them thought it was a great idea—until I asked them to send me a paragraph of their news by a specific date. My experiment quickly turned into an exercise in patience, a crash course in communicating with millennials, and considerable instruction and encouragement to help my grandkids understand the difference between "routine" and "boring." Slowly but surely they're all doing it; they're contributing, commenting and responding to each other. All it requires is grandparents taking the initiative and gently and firmly leading younger people to fulfill their commitments—and to do it on time!

I am sure that some grandparents are reluctant to take initiatives with their adult grandchildren, either through fear that they will not relate to each other or that the young people will be too busy. But pleasant surprises await grandparents who reach out to their grandchildren. Jill and I keep a huge unfinished jigsaw puzzle on our dining room table that is slowly and laboriously taking shape, and it has proven a magnet for grandchildren. One recent evening, when those who live in Milwaukee were visiting, we invited the grandkids over. All who were free came (along with a fiancée, some significant others and some not-yet-as-significant others), and after food, we all descended on the puzzle for a couple of hours! The bonding was palpable, the joshing was relentless and the chatter was nonstop. While all this was going on, I played some "Poppa music" (Mozart, to be precise); and they actually began to comment on this music, which they normally never would have listened to. Eventually they went on their ways, but one of my granddaughters wrote in the monthly newsletter that the evening spent doing a jigsaw puzzle together and listening to Poppa's music was the highlight of her visit home. Surprise, surprise!

These examples highlight one of the major roles of grandparents: being available. Availability and accessibility are things that we can and should offer the younger generation. This requires grandparents to make a conscious effort to show interest in grandkids, to struggle to understand them and to remain consistently in touch. As seniors, we benefit by being reminded that we have value, and we are given a chance to be rejuvenated by mixing with the younger crowd. The younger generation finds in their grandparents a resource of experienced, trustworthy guidance and sees a model of firm and seasoned faithfulness. If they choose to listen, they may hear words of timely encouragement, the wisdom of age and even healthy correction. Connecting with the younger generation requires an ability to listen, a willingness to keep our mouth shut, a determined effort to try to understand, a suspension of critical evaluation, an acceptance of the inevitable and a dash of patience. The rising generation, in our experience, responds to this kind of grandparent; and if all goes well, the day may come when a granddaughter, newly arrived home from college, calls us and says, "May I bring my boyfriend over? He's really cute, and he wants to meet you. I've told him all about you, and I hope you like him. And can we light a fire, and would you make shepherd's pie like you used to when we were kids, please?" No grandparent I know is going to be too busy, tired, out of touch, or preoccupied to respond positively to such an opportunity! When the young people arrive, we find that they just want to "hang," which as far as I can determine means being together and not saying much. They stay long past our bedtime.

When we ask our grandkids what we can pray for them about, they will answer frankly and honestly, because they want us to pray for them. They count on us being in touch with heaven on their behalf, even when they may not be so themselves. Parenting is for life, although it changes with the seasons, and grandparenting offers and involves a parallel involvement.

Let me encourage those of you without grandchildren to recognize that many young people desperately need a grandparent figure in their lives. Go look for them, and take the initiative to reach out to them. You may be surprised by their reaction. Jill and I were recently surprised when a young female nurse, upon completing her second tour of duty with the US Marines in Iraq, e-mailed us from overseas and said, "My grandmother just passed away, and I'm appointing you two as my honorary grandparents, because I'm far too young not to have grandparents in my life." By my reckoning, if she's too young to do without grandparents, that means that Jill and I are not too old to stand with her, be available to her, listen to her, encourage her and advise her when she asks for advice. She just needs us to be there! We need to sharpen all these skills; but as we work on them, the result should be some degree of improving with age.

For Personal Reflection and Group Discussion

Points to Ponder

- Grandparenting is so much fun that if we'd known it, we'd have had grandkids first.
- Connecting with the younger generation requires an ability to listen, a willingness to keep our mouth shut, a determined effort to try to understand, a suspension of critical evaluation, an acceptance of the inevitable and a dash of patience.
- When our grandchildren become young adults, our relationship with them changes; it is still capable of producing a lot of fun, but it can also bring its share of heartaches, concerns and disappointments, and it can require adjustments.
- One of the major roles of grandparents is being available. Availability and accessibility are things we can and should offer the younger generation.
- Some grandparents are reluctant to take initiative with their adult grandchildren, either through fear that they will not relate to each other or that the young people will be too busy.
- Our grandchildren count on us being in touch with heaven on their behalf, even when they may not be so themselves.

Discuss/Journal/Pray

1. Spend some time reflecting on the Points to Ponder.
2. How can you work to develop a relationship with your grandkids?
3. What ideas from this chapter might you try with your own grandkids?
4. Pray for your kids and grandkids who are struggling with moral values that seem to them to be from another planet. Do you need to learn their language? How do you do that?
5. Idea: start a class at church or in a home in which kids and grandkids can teach the older generation how to e-mail, tweet or use Facebook.
6. What joys of aging have you discovered as you have been a part of your grandchildren's lives?

A Personal Note from Jill

In your community, there are older people who would love to be grandparents but who, for one reason or another, are not. You will also find younger people who would love to have a grandparent but have none. In light of Stuart's and my experience with Melissa, which he mentioned in this chapter, we recommend that people without grandchildren or grandparents explore the possibility of "adopting" or "being adopted."

Maybe you are in this situation. Why don't you begin praying about how God might use you in the life of someone who is missing the love, wisdom and input of a grandparent? **No Greater Joy**

John the apostle, having heard some very good news from his "dear friend Gaius" whom "He loved in truth," wrote of his spiritual children, "I have no greater joy than to hear that my children are walking in the truth" (3 John 4). We can't buy that! Spiritual, exuberant joy is ours when our children and grandchildren, natural or spiritual, walk in the truth, love the Lord, obey the Lord and, joy of joys, serve the Lord! To this great end we pray!

No greater joy when my children walk in truth,
No greater sorrow when they don't;
No greater joy when they love the Lord I love,
No greater heartbreak when they won't!
No greater joy when persistent prayer is answered,
No greater privilege to pray—
No greater work as we fight the battle for them,
Trusting He will answer one great day.

No greater joy when they tell us they are praying,
Reading the Word and digging in,
No greater news when they choose a godly lifestyle,
No greater battle can they win—
No greater wonder when we watch the Holy Spirit
Power and equip them for their days,
And no greater joy, when they'll stand with us in Glory
As we offer our Lord Jesus all the Praise!

No greater joy when my children walk in truth,
No greater sorrow when they don't.
No greater joy when they love the Lord that I love,
No greater heartbreak when they won't![1]

Pray for your kids and grandkids to walk in truth, and pray about how God might use you as a grandparent to encourage their faith.

20

GRUMPY OLD MEN

I rarely watch Hollywood movies. In fact, I occasionally read reviews to save myself from having to watch the movie. I do know that most movies are made for the under-forty crowd, with the exception of movies that target those under twenty-five. That being the case, not a lot of work is available for aging actors other than stereotypical cameo roles as grandmas and grandpas.

Occasionally, however, veteran actors are called upon to star in a movie about senior citizens. One such movie produced years ago was *Grumpy Old Men*. This is one of the movies that I have not seen, but the title points to another stereotype of aged people in Hollywood movies: older people get grumpier as the years go by!

I have no doubt that there is some truth to this perception, and there may be some justification for some older people being something considerably less than Mr. or Mrs. Conviviality. A lot of them don't feel well. It doesn't matter how old we are if we are aching from head to toe; when we are, our attitude is easily affected.

Then there's the difficulty that older people experience as we try to manage the degree and speed of change around us. Life becomes confusing when we don't know how things work, what things mean and what's expected of us. My mother never felt at home using a telephone. Telephones of the landline variety have mainly gone the way of the dodo, and now my cell phone tells me where I am and how to get where I'm going. It actually talks to me in a soothing female voice. It takes my photographs and sends them across the world to my Facebook page, where the pictures go viral in minutes. It allows me to watch Manchester United play on the other side of the world; it stores my notes and reminds me of my appointments; and, if I want to listen to a Welsh, male-voice choir, it will bring one up for me in seconds and transport me to the valleys of South Wales in an instant. How would my mother have coped with an iPhone? This changing world is disorienting for the elderly, and the result is marginalization and confusion, so "grumpy" can take over.

Jean, a dear friend of mine, served as a missionary in Eastern Congo for forty years before being forced to retire at age seventy. She returned to the United States to live with her son and his wife. One day, shortly after arriving, she was asked to pick up a can of applesauce from the supermarket on her way home. She found her way through the maze of displays to the correct department and started to work along the lines of many variegated applesauces. The more she saw, the more confused she became. She had no idea that applesauce came in so many cans, bottles, flavors and colors, both sweetened and unsweetened. She had no idea what to choose, was concerned that she would pick the wrong variety, and wasn't used to having a cell phone handy to call home and inquire, so she eventually rushed from the supermarket in tears and drove home without the applesauce!

Bear in mind that this lady had served as a missionary widow in the African bush for decades. She had lived through life-threatening revolutions, lost everything on two separate occasions, and sailed through it all with rare good grace and humor. But she could not cope with the ever-changing pace and variety in the world that had somehow appeared, uninvited and unappreciated, on her doorstep. She was singularly unprepared, frightened, insecure and living on the edge.

The question for Jean and others like her of this world is, how can we improve our ability to cope with the changes that are happening all around us without becoming grumpy?

I've noticed that in America it is customary to greet people with a cheery, "How are you?" without waiting for a response. In Britain a common response to "How are you?" is "Not so bad." If you're not expecting too much, what you get doesn't seem all that bad, so "Not so bad" does just fine! My old friend John Dixon, whom I used to meet most mornings on my way to the office, used to invariably respond to my cheery greeting with, "Can't grumble," usually followed immediately with some good-natured grumbling. "Can't grumble" is a slightly more detailed response than "Not so bad."

Grumbling doesn't change very many situations. I doubt if it makes grumblers any happier, and I'm certain that it makes everyone subjected to it most unhappy. "Counterproductive" is, therefore, the best way to describe this all-too-common practice.

Perhaps we can learn from the Brits. Their approach to life includes avoiding disappointment by not pinning their hopes on something that experience has told them is unlikely to happen. For instance, if they don't expect the sun to shine tomorrow, they won't be disappointed if it doesn't, and they won't need to grumble about it. This attitude can certainly be applied to disappointments about change and our difficulties in adjusting to and accepting it. The unavoidable fact is that change happens, is happening and will no doubt continue to happen! If we don't expect everything to be the same as it was when we were young(er)—because it will never be like that again—we won't be as disappointed when things change. That will be one less thing to grumble about, one less reason to be grumpy! It's called acceptance.

It's not a matter of accepting what you find totally unacceptable—to do that would mean suspending your ability to evaluate, compromising principles and adopting unpalatable positions. If your grandchild decides to live with his girlfriend without the commitment of marriage, which you are convinced is necessary, that will be troubling for you. So what does acceptance mean in that situation? It doesn't mean that you ought to say, "Oh, well. Times have changed. I guess I need to change my way of looking at things as well. After all, they all seem to be doing that nowadays." But it does mean that we must accept the unavoidable fact that this "new morality"—which is actually a very old one in modern dress—is here and probably here to stay for a while, and to go on laboring the point that we disapprove of it will serve no useful purpose.

But if you believe that young people are getting it wrong and need to learn where they are going wrong, then grandparents are some of the best people to get the message across. This is best done not through a grumpy lecture but through a mode of approach and address that shows that we at least understand where they are coming from and where they're probably heading! We may tell them that we recognize that setting up a home is too expensive for them at present, that they can't afford the kind of weddings their parents had, that their job situation is tenuous, and that they've been "seeing each other" for years so we understand why they want to be together and why they think that living together is the best solution. We can sympathize with their position but not their solution. We can give them our reasons if they want to hear them. (Incidentally, there is a much greater chance that they will be open to hearing what we have to say if our approach to them is loving and caring.) We may be able to suggest ways to help them—and perhaps become in some measure part of the solution.

This is how we can improve with age and improve in our grandparenting at the same time. No grumbling, no grumpy old men (or women)—just old-timers who've seen a thing or two, know a couple of things, stand for a lot of things, love their grandkids and are doing their very best in a difficult situation!

For Personal Reflection and Group Discussion

Points to Ponder

- The movie title *Grumpy Old Men* points to the stereotype of aged people in Hollywood movies: older people get grumpier as the years go by.
- If we are aching from head to toe, our attitude can easily be affected.

- This changing world is disorienting for the elderly, and the result is marginalization and confusion, so "grumpy" can take over.
- Grumbling doesn't change very many situations. I doubt if it makes grumblers any happier, and I'm certain that it makes everyone subjected to it most unhappy. "Counterproductive" is the best way to describe this all-too-common practice.
- If we don't expect everything to be the same as it was when we were young(er)—because it will never be like that again—we won't be disappointed when things change. That will be one less thing to grumble about, one less reason to be grumpy! It's called acceptance.

Discuss/Journal/Pray

1. Spend some time reflecting on the Points to Ponder.
2. How can we improve our ability to cope with the changes that are happening all around us without becoming grumpy?
3. Make a list of the changes that you find most difficult. Think of ways to address them so that you stand by your principles *and* adjust where able.
4. How can accepting the changes in this stage of life keep you from falling into the grumbling rut?
5. Seek advice from others who have faced the problems you are facing. Then pray that the Lord grants you patience, courage and help.

A Personal Note from Jill

There is an alternative to becoming a grumpy old person. A psychologist friend of ours calls it "the grace to be diminished." Win Couchman picked up on this phrase and wrote,

> Even though my husband Bob and I have sat in the balcony of our church for forty years or so, sitting there has concerned me for the past several years. There are no railings up there, and the steep incline of the balcony meant that the back of the seats in front of us were too far down to lean against. But those were our seats, and around us were all our many pew friends. How could we ever move down to the floor level?
>
> Then my beloved older sister fell; a dreadful full-length fall backwards onto asphalt. Three days later she died. Bob and I spoke to each other after that about how, when one is old, in many situations one must either act foolishly or look foolish. It may be wise to walk more slowly, carry a cane, whatever. Even if it looks sort of foolish to onlookers, to be prudent, we must change our ways to match our season. We needed grace to be diminished. So we moved to the main floor of the church.[1]

21

HINDSIGHT, INSIGHT AND FORESIGHT

Tevye, the milkman, was the central character of the re-cord-breaking Broadway musical *Fiddler on the Roof*. The musical is based on Chagall's painting *The Fiddler* which represents the joyous, irrepressible way in which Eastern European Jews have endured untold hardships through their faith and traditions. The movie's title points out that the violinist, while still playing, is doing so in a very precarious position—perched on a roof! This is illustrated in the sad story of Tevye, the dirt-poor persecuted Russian Jew who struggles to cope with the inhumane edicts of his czarist rulers, crushing poverty and the way his three oldest daughters trample his traditions.

As Tevye confronts what, in his mind, is one long series of disasters, he tries to come to terms with each situation by using a familiar pattern: "on the one hand" he lists things in favor of granting his daughters' wishes, but "on the other hand" he sees no possibility of doing so. As the musical progresses, we become accustomed to his "on the one hand, on the other hand" way of coping—until the final straw comes. His youngest daughter wants to marry a Christian, and this challenges not only Tevye's traditions but his faith as well. He reverts to his well-worn way of reasoning, "On the one hand"—then he pauses and almost howls, "*There is no other hand!*"

The ability to see one hand of a situation and also the other hand and then to weigh them both comes with *experience*. But having done that, the strength to say, "There is no other hand!" when the occasion demands it comes from *conviction*. Aging provides us many opportunities to garner experience and formulate conviction.

Experience grants us the privilege of seeing and experiencing, of benefitting from or being subjected to, events and movements that before long will have had their day and will probably pass into the shadows of general forgetfulness—except in the minds of those who have gone through the events. Those who experience don't forget; they know what happened, and they store it in their memories. Then when another development comes along, they store it alongside the ones they still remember from former days. If they make an effort, they can balance the two and become people who recognize trends. Hindsight, through their experiences, begets insight and foresight.

Since they know what has transpired, these people have an idea of what may happen again; and if they project that into the future, they may be able to give wise advice on the feasibility of the new development. Trends have beginnings that can easily be overlooked in the immediacy of a new development or the enthusiasm of a movement. The ones who have no knowledge or experience of the former days may, with every good intention, stumble into repeating the mistakes of their predecessors. It's those who have lived through former days, have gained experience, and have the ability to speak from that experience into the contemporary scene who have invaluable insights to offer. This is one of the things the aged can do well! Paul Tournier wrote in *Learning to Grow Old*, "Life is movement, evolution, progression, not stagnation; it can be comprehended only in its incessant becoming, in its total continuity. You need a sense of history if you are to make sense of life."[1]

It is well known that Winston Churchill foresaw the danger of the rising Nazi party in Germany long before his colleagues recognized it. But he also foresaw halfway through World War II, after the United States joined the Allies, that Germany was—or would be—defeated, and he stated then that the Soviet Union was not to be trusted. He based this prediction on his knowledge of history. He explained that Napoleon was defeated at Waterloo because he did not recognize the danger the British posed to him and so was preoccupied with the Prussians. Churchill concluded that if the Allies focused solely on defeating the Nazis without recognizing the growing threat posed by the Soviets, the Allies would be in danger of being defeated eventually not by the Germans but by the Russians. That is to say, Napoleon would not be the only person to meet his Waterloo.

It also follows that if experience flashes warning signals that, when carefully examined, prove to be warnings of potential disaster, or at least of avoidable mistakes, then older people are the ones who have something of value to say. They may be in a position to advise, "On the one hand, I can see the value of A, and on the other hand there is no doubt something to be gained from B; but the factor that is inescapable is C, and since this is nonnegotiable, this is no-go territory." In other words, there is no other hand in this case! We call that conviction, and in a world in which sentiment is much easier to dispense and much more readily accepted, conviction is in short supply.

Experience and conviction are not limited solely to those who have lived a long time, but chances are that those who have lived a long time will have experienced more than those who have not; therefore, those who have lived a long time will have had more opportunity to balance experience against experience and arrive at more viable convictions. This can improve the balanced thinking of the older ones as well as the information they are capable of sharing. Improving with age!

For Personal Reflection and Group Discussion

Points to Ponder

- The ability to see one hand of a situation and also the other hand and to weigh them both comes with *experience*. Aging provides us many opportunities to garner experience and formulate *convictions*.

- "You need a sense of history if you want to make sense of life" (Paul Tournier).

- If experience flashes warning signals that, when carefully examined, prove to be warnings of potential disaster, or at least avoidable mistakes, then it follows that older people are the ones who have something of value to say.

- In a world in which sentiment is much easier to dispense and much more readily accepted, conviction is in short supply.
- Experience and conviction are not limited solely to those who have lived a long time.

Discuss/Journal/Pray

1. Spend some time reflecting on the Points to Ponder.
2. Discuss how hard it is to dispense advice to a new generation that seems to know little of our world.
3. How does this chapter encourage you that you have valuable things to say and contribute and that you have experience from which others need to draw?

A Personal Note from Jill

Some time ago, an odd trend suddenly appeared in the youth culture. Young men began wearing their blue jeans as if they were about to drop off their bodies. Conspicuously displayed sliding pants were adorned with brightly colored undershorts. Apart from looking untidy, the fashion looked desperately uncomfortable and definitely precarious.

On asking our young friends why their peers were dressing in this fashion, the best explanation we received was, "Everybody's doing it. It's cool." We were aware, however, that the "fashion statement" originated in the inner city, where a high percentage of the young men were in trouble with the law. Some of them even ended up in prison; there they were not allowed to wear belts, so their pants hung down low. What our young people called "cool" was actually a statement of solidarity with young criminals in prison.

It helps if older people take the trouble to use their experience to formulate opinions and then share them with young people who may know nothing more than which trend to follow.

22

ALONE OR LONELY?

Recent estimates show that thirty-one million Americans now live alone. That is close to one-quarter of all households. Some are alone by choice. Some enjoy active social lives and cherish the chance to go home to be by themselves. Others choose to be alone in virtual isolation because they dislike or even fear social contact. Some live alone through no fault of their own and no desire on their part, perhaps as a result of family dissolution or bereavement.

A year or two ago, I met an old California gold miner who lives not far from Yosemite. Sitting with him in his shack on the edge of a crystal clear stream in a narrow gulch, drinking bitter coffee in a tin cup, it would have been easy to imagine that he and I were the only people left on the planet. Apparently the miner had settled in the area decades before, eked out a living panning for gold and was perfectly happy being by himself. He welcomed an occasional individual visit from a small group of friends so long as they didn't stay too long! Living without radio or television and as a total stranger to computers, he had minimal knowledge—or concern—about world affairs. His main concerns seemed to be forest fires and drought. He had a few dusty old books and one well-worn, well-thumbed old Bible that he read to us using battered old spectacles missing a lens.

The words "alone" and lonely" are often used together and perhaps even interchangeably, but they speak to different issues. There are certainly connections between the two, but the difference needs to be understood. It is possible to be alone without being lonely. My miner friend was certainly alone and marginally isolated but not lonely. He appeared to be well-adjusted to his chosen lifestyle and perfectly happy doing what he did. Alone, yes; lonely, no. On the other hand, it is possible to be lonely even in the midst of a crowd. Young people arriving on a campus for the first time, surrounded by thousands of lively young people, will feel pangs of loneliness in the midst of a crowd. I have been in many meetings in which hundreds of people are congregated in noisy fellowship, and I've noted the quiet individual sitting alone, uncomfortable, ill at ease and desperately lonely. And perhaps most surprising, caregivers report that some of the most lonely people they meet do not live alone but with a married or unmarried partner. Alone, no; lonely, yes.

What exactly is loneliness? Search through books and websites of quotations, and you will find as many descriptions as authors. Mother Teresa said, "Loneliness and the feeling of being unwanted is the most terrible poverty."[1] Spending her life as she did in the slums of Calcutta, she would know! Those slums have to be seen to be believed. They teem with a mass of humanity like no other place on earth that I have visited. There no one is ever alone. Seclusion and solitude do not exist in that place, but "the feeling of being unwanted" pervades the foul air. Many of the people own only the rags on their backs, sleep on the filthy sidewalks, eat from refuse bins and "bathe" under a faucet in full view of the disinterested masses. When they are sick, they lie untended; when they die, they lie where they fall. The poverty is palpable. But note what Mother Teresa said: "Loneliness . . . is the most terrible poverty." It's a feeling that no one cares, that nothing matters and that hope is dying. Sadness like a heavy cloud blankets the soul.

This feeling, however, like many others, may have no basis in fact. Contrary to what a person's emotions say, he or she may have those who care, may have things of value still to be done. Where there's life, there really is hope—and God has promised to be with us.

Remember that this sorry state is common among the retired and elderly population both inside and outside the community of faith. If we are guilty of marginalizing the seniors in our midst, we are probably creating situations in which feelings of loneliness can take root and grow. A ministry of presence is called for!

There is, however, another side to the coin—if aloneness does not automatically lead to loneliness, what else can it lead to? Turning to Scripture, we quickly see the richness and fullness of life that is available to the believer who uses time alone wisely and well. The prime example, of course, is the lifestyle of our Lord. The Gospels are full of references to His practice of intentional solitude. He was often alone; but, with the exception of His extraordinary cry from the cross, "My God, my God, why have you forsaken me?" (Matt. 27:46), He gave no indication of ever being lonely. He clearly delighted in solitude, and by His repeated practice of getting away, He showed how vital it was to His communion with the Father (see Matt. 4:1–11; 14:13; 17:1–9; 26:36–46). Richard Foster wrote, "Loneliness is inner emptiness. Solitude is inner fulfillment."[2]

Solitude and silence are first cousins, and we all know the scarcity of silence in our world—except, perhaps, when alone in a senior living home. In 1807, long before the days of all-pervasive electronic music, traffic jams, low-flying aircraft, lawnmowers and cell phones, Wordsworth wrote, "The world is too much with us."[3] Ironically, while many need to turn their loneliness into solitude, many others need to escape the crowds and the din and "be still, and know that [He is] God" (Ps. 46:10).

This will never happen without conscious effort. Those who are lonely have no problem finding quietness, but it often serves to point their minds and feelings in the direction of their sorrows and disappointments. They need to make a conscious effort to turn their thoughts heavenward. But for those for whom stillness and quietness are hard to find, inner stillness can be practiced through such activities as running, walking, driving and eating lunch. Those seeking to cultivate stillness have to decide to make the effort and stick with it! It helps to have a set time, a specific place or a regular pattern for solitude; but as we saw earlier in our reflections on reading, Scripture and prayer, our time of quiet to focus on the things of heaven can be had anywhere on earth, using the many means that God has graciously provided.

I learned a long time ago that upsides have downsides, and we should be aware of both. Solitude that leads to spiritual communion with the Lord and fellowship with believers in worship and service are clearly upsides of being alone! The downside of solitude or aloneness is that it can slide into loneliness. The right kind of fellowship counters that possibility—but the downside of fellowship is that it can be little more than having a good time with friends. The depth of devotion that comes from solitude adds content to relationships. Richard Foster has a wise word for us on this topic: "We must seek out the recreating stillness of solitude if we want to be with others meaningfully. We must seek the fellowship and accountability of others if we want to be alone safely. We must cultivate both if we are to live in obedience."[4]

For Personal Reflection and Group Discussion

Points to Ponder

- It is possible to be alone without being lonely. It is possible to be lonely even in the midst of a crowd.
- "Loneliness and the feeling of being unwanted is the most terrible poverty" (Mother Teresa).
- Turning to Scripture, we quickly see the richness and fullness of life that is available to the believer who uses time alone wisely and well.
- Richard Foster wrote, "Loneliness is inner emptiness. Solitude is inner fulfillment."
- Stillness and quietness are hard to find, but inner stillness can be practiced through such activities as running, walking, driving and eating lunch.
- Our time of quiet to focus on the things of heaven can be had from anywhere on earth.

Discuss/Journal/Pray

1. Spend some time reflecting on the Points to Ponder.
2. Discuss the difference between aloneness and loneliness.
3. Look up Matthew 14:23; Mark 1:35; 6:46; Luke 5:16; 6:12. What do these verses tell us about Jesus' use of solitude?
4. How can you apply these Scriptures to yourself and others?
5. How can Scripture, prayer and times of quiet help you focus on things of heaven?
6. Pray about this.

A Personal Note from Jill

Do you ever get really heart hungry for the people you love? Maybe your children are divorced, and you lost your grandchildren when their parents moved a continent away. Or perhaps your Mom died when you were young, and you've had a mother hole in your heart ever since. Or like me, maybe your work separates you from your loved ones on an ongoing basis. I have always had someone missing in my life:

> "I've lived my life always missing someone," I reflected as I said goodbye to my husband one more time and got ready to climb on one more plane for one more flight for one more engagement.
>
> When I'm down, I start to feel sorry for myself. I was down that day as I saw my husband off to the back of beyond in Mali, West Africa, and as I waited for my plane back to the States.

I boarded the plane weeping quietly into my Coke and wondered what to do. I could have a pity party all by myself, or I could think about Jesus. I struggled. The thing about a pity party is that we don't need to go to the trouble of inviting anyone—we can wallow in things all by ourselves.

"Lord, you've been in Mali?" I began, stopping abruptly at the silliness of that remark. I knew that He loved Africa! He sat down beside me.

"I was thinking," I began eagerly, now that I had His full attention. "I seem to have lived my life always missing someone."

"I understand," He interrupted my flood of words. "I feel just as you do every one of your 'man' days, Jill. I'm always missing someone. I'm missing all the people I died for, who chose not to come home to Me." I was stunned. I'd never thought of that.[5]

- Think about how God understands your loneliness.
- Who are the people you are heart hungry for?
- How can missing someone make you feel lonely?
- What can you do in those moments of loneliness to avoid a pity party?

23

PAUL, THE AGED

P aul's letter to Philemon is brief, to the point and frequently overlooked. That is a pity, because in it Paul describes himself as "Paul—an old man" (9). When I recognized this, I became particularly interested in studying how Paul seemed to be dealing with his aging.

As I read through the letter, it was immediately obvious that Paul was not only getting on in years; he was also a "prisoner of Christ Jesus . . . in chains" (1, 10) He was in prison! Incidentally, we believe that Paul was approximately sixty years of age when he described himself as an old man—something that few self-respecting, modern sixty-year-olds would do. So let's see what we can learn from one of our fellow aging believers, who was living in circumstances that most of us have never experienced and hopefully never will.

Paul, while in prison, probably in Rome, found himself dealing with a runaway slave who was the "property" of his good friend and fellow believer Philemon, a respected citizen and church leader in Colosse (the church to whom Paul addressed the epistle to the Colossians). I suppose Paul could have said, "I'm an old man, and this young guy is nothing but trouble. At my age, I don't need it!" But he didn't. He took the desperate man under his wing, and eventually, through Paul's ministry, the runaway slave, Onesimus, became a committed and rapidly maturing follower of Jesus.

Paul's behavior at this point reveals the lie in the oft-repeated senior statement, "I've done my bit. I don't need more responsibility. I've earned my rest. Let the younger ones pick up the load." In this case, it is doubtful if anyone other than a respected older man, preferably one who was on good terms with Philemon, could have talked to Philemon as Paul did or could have asked him to take the action that he requested. Younger individuals are ideally suited to do things that older people are no longer capable of handling, but that should not obscure the fact that they are not always equipped to pick up the loads that some old-timers would like to bequeath to them!

Paul was undoubtedly well acquainted with the law stated in Deuteronomy, "You shall not give up to his master a slave who has escaped from his master to you. He shall dwell with you, in your midst, in the place that he shall choose within one of your towns, wherever it suits him. You shall not wrong him" (23:15–16, ESV). Athenian law went even further and stipulated that a slave in danger of his life could seek sanctuary with a private family, and the head of that family must protect him and seek reconciliation for him with his master. This is in sharp contrast to other legislation—not uncommon in Roman culture—that mandated execution not only for the runaway but also for those who harbored him![1]

We are not told how Onesimus found Paul or even if they had been previously acquainted with each other, but it is possible that the runaway slave went to Paul seeking sanctuary and looking for an advocate. Whether or not that is how they came to meet under such unlikely circumstances, that is precisely what Onesimus got, and much more!

Paul faced a life-and-death decision. Would he hand over Onesimus, possibly to be executed, or would he go to bat for him? Washing his hands of the young man would save Paul a lot of time and trouble—but it could cost the young man his life! Paul had more than enough problems of his own; aiding the man would involve him in all manner of challenges and responsibilities.

The apostle chose to take on the burden of the young man's predicament. More than that, he recognized Onesimus' spiritual needs and so ministered the gospel to him in word and deed that the young renegade came to a living faith. And the apostle's ministry to the young convert did not end there. Under Paul's careful nurturing, the new believer rapidly developed into a mature follower of Jesus. The apostle's ringing endorsement of the runaway beautifully describes how much Onesimus had grown in the Lord. Paul described him as "a dear brother," saying, "[he] is my very heart," and admitted, "I would have liked to keep him with me so that he could take your place in helping me while I am in chains for the gospel" (see Philem. 12–16).

Paul was well able in his advancing years to take risks, make hard decisions, accept new responsibilities, minister across the generations and disciple a younger man from a culture different from his own. He was in touch with the issues of his day and willing to be involved in them and make wise decisions about them. Paul's example in prison presents all aging people with a challenge and a model of mature servanthood. Perhaps we can quote him out of context: "Follow my example, as I follow the example of Christ" (1 Cor. 11:1).

For Personal Reflection and Group Discussion

Points to Ponder

- "I've done my bit. I don't need more responsibility. I've earned my rest. Let the younger ones pick up the load."
- The apostle chose to take on the burden of the young man's predicament. More than that, he recognized Onesimus' spiritual needs and so ministered the gospel to him in word and deed that the young renegade came to a living faith. And the apostle's ministry to the young convert did not end there. Under Paul's careful nurturing, the new believer rapidly developed into a mature follower of Jesus.
- Paul was well able in his advancing years to take risks, make hard decisions, accept new responsibilities, minister across the generations and disciple a younger man from a culture different from his own. He was in touch with the issues of his day and was willing to be involved in them and make wise decisions about them.

Discuss/Journal/Pray

1. Spend some time reflecting on the Points to Ponder.

2. There are many ways we can read Paul's letter to Philemon with great profit, but as we are focusing on improving with age, let us see what we can learn about Paul's attitudes and activities in his old age. Make a list of these.

3. How was Paul, as an old man, still being used by God in younger people's lives?

4. In what ways can you be involved in mentoring the younger people in your life?

5. In another context Paul wrote, "Follow my example, as I follow the example of Christ" (1 Cor. 11:1).

   • How did Paul's behavior in prison emulate Christ's example?

   • How do you need to apply Paul's example to your situation?

A Personal Note from Jill

When I was nineteen years old, I had a run-in with an illness that required a period of rehabilitation. The only place available was a retirement home for elderly people, so I was sent there, and I wasn't very happy about it! I asked if I could talk with a chaplain, but I was told that no chaplain visited the retirement home. I got a similar negative response to an inquiry about a Sunday service. My unhappiness degenerated into a sulky pity party.

Until I had an idea! Instead of feeling sorry for myself, perhaps I could bring a message to my fellow bored and lonely "inmates." On inquiry, I finally got a positive answer: "That would be lovely, dear. You can have a wheelchair, and we'll wheel in the rest of the patients." It was not on par with Paul the prisoner and Onesimus the runaway slave, but it was a start in learning to serve in less-than-ideal circumstances. We can all do that!

24

FRIENDS: GOD'S GIFT TO MANKIND

P aul, as an experienced missionary, knew full well that leading someone to faith is only the beginning. Leading a new believer into mature faith takes much time and effort. There are many challenges and heartaches in dealing with the baggage that new believers often bring into their new experience of Christ. Such was the case with Onesimus. This young man faced a possible death sentence; but by giving him sanctuary, Paul was morally required to engage in potentially difficult mediatorial negotiations. These involved asking his old friend Philemon to ignore the legal prescriptions for punishing the runaway slave and to accept him as a mature believer in Christ into the community of faith in Colosse.

It is not difficult to imagine how Paul's request might have caused controversy, even among the believers in the church that met in Philemon's home (see Philem. 1–2). Assuming that both Hebrew and Gentile believers with differing legal and political convictions were meeting together, it is possible that they could, and would, take opposing positions on how Onesimus should be treated. It is possible that Gentile slave owners in Colosse would be outraged if Philemon acceded to Paul's request by being lenient—by receiving the renegade as a brother in Christ. They might see this as an undermining of their hard-line, law-and-order way of keeping slaves in their place. (Years ago, when I frequently traveled in South Africa during the sad days of apartheid, I saw firsthand the depth of division among Christians and the bitterness of their disagreements on legal and political matters.)

Old-man Paul was probably well aware of what might happen as a result of his intervention. We all know that even in the church, racial, ethnic and cultural differences can wreak havoc, and political differences can split a church wide open. Having spent many years personally dealing with no-win situations in church life, I could easily imagine Paul thinking that it might be better for his blood pressure if he ducked this issue and sent Onesimus away. But he didn't. He embraced the young man in his need, ministered to him to great effect, and eventually sat down and wrote his famous letter to Philemon. He waded into the situation with eyes wide open and a heart full of compassion. Based on Paul's profound conviction that showed him what he *ought* to do and well-nurtured relationships that made it possible for him to do what he *needed* to do, he wrote his letter.

The letter's tone is warm and friendly—and straightforward! Paul calls Philemon "our dear friend" (1) and writes to him, "Your love has given me great joy and encouragement, because you, brother, have refreshed the hearts of the Lord's people" (7). The letter also includes formal introductions of and greetings from colleagues whom Paul describes as "partner," "fellow worker," "fellow prisoner," and "fellow soldier." But the issues he raises are addressed firmly and directly. He needed help, support and encouragement; and his relationships were of such a quality that he could ask for aid without embarrassment and with the confidence that well-established, loving friendships would carry the day in a difficult situation.

It is obvious that over the years, despite, or perhaps because of, his arduous travel schedule, Paul had nurtured deep relationships. And in his own time of need, he had no hesitation in calling for help from those who loved him. At the same time, he exercised leadership and called his friends to follow his example. That's what friends are for—particularly friends who can truthfully be called brother or sister, as Philemon and Apphia were (see Philem. 2, 7).

Friendship, partnership and fellowship of this kind don't develop overnight. It takes time, work, sacrifice, commitment and desire. This kind of time involvement is possible for those of us with some time on our hands.

Over the years, it is possible for relationships to deteriorate or disintegrate altogether. Maybe our later years can be productively invested in mending fences, repairing damage and healing old hurts. In situations in which nothing quite so serious as a fractured relationship is the case, if relationships have drifted apart because of busyness (or business), they could easily be restored and enriched by a well-placed phone call or a well-written letter.

Let me say a word or two about letter writing. These days, letter writing is rapidly following the dodo into extinction; and in its place we have texts, tweets, posts and other wonders of social media. Media they certainly are, but whether or not they deserve the appellation "social" is debatable. I know that e-mails and texts and similar technological innovations make for quick, easy, accessible communication—and I use them constantly—but they are limited. Marshall McLuhan famously told us, "The medium is the message," something that I never understood until I read Neil Postman's wonderful book *Amusing Ourselves to Death*. Postman pointed out that "the medium is the message" means that the mode of communication shapes and even limits the communication that results. He wrote, "While I do not know what content was once carried in the smoke signals of American Indians, I can safely guess it did not include philosophical argument. . . . You cannot use smoke to do philosophy. Its form excludes the content."[1] In the same way, letters, as they used to be written, provide a means of careful, meaningful communication that today's media cannot offer. As a result, our communication is often limited, and our relationships suffer.

Paul teaches us many things in his letter to Philemon. Two of them are that we should take time to develop deep friendships and that we should write letters to communicate in an in-depth manner with our friends. These are two more things we can do to make leisure productive!

For Personal Reflection and Group Discussion

Points to Ponder

- Paul needed help, support and encouragement; and his relationships were of such a quality that he could ask for aid without embarrassment and with the confidence that well-established, loving friendships would carry the day in a difficult situation.

- It is obvious that over the years, despite his arduous travel schedule, Paul had nurtured deep relationships. In his time of need, he had no hesitation in calling for help from those who loved him.

- Over the years, it is possible for relationships to deteriorate or disintegrate altogether. Maybe our later years can be invested productively in mending fences, repairing damage and healing old hurts.

- Paul teaches us many things in his letter to Philemon. Two of them are that we should take time to develop deep friendships and that we should write letters to communicate in an in-depth manner with our friends.

Discuss/Journal/Pray

1. Spend some time reflecting on the Points to Ponder.
2. We know that relationships can deteriorate or disintegrate; but the good news is that in later years, we can invest in mending fences and making other necessary repairs. (For more on this, maybe look up a Scripture or two on forgiveness and discuss what you find.)

3. Look up the following verses on forgiveness: Matt. 6:12–15; 18:21–22, 35; Col. 3:13. With whom do you need to mend fences?
4. Where do you need to start? Write a letter? Make a phone call? Perhaps even write on a Facebook wall or two!
5. Pray about this, and make a plan to repair relationship damage and heal old hurts.

A Personal Note from Jill

When our children were small, a friend of ours lived with us while she did her missionary training. After leaving our home, she served for many years as a single missionary in Austria. We maintained contact with her over the years and eventually were saddened to hear that she was suffering from cancer.

One day we received a letter from her telling us that she knew she did not have long to live and that she was spending her remaining days making sure that her relationships were as they ought to be. She was writing to everyone she felt she may have offended. Accordingly, she wanted to apologize for taking some trivial articles from our home many years previously—articles that we had never missed! Her conscience in later days was clearly deeply sensitive; she did what she needed to do. She used her later years well!

Spilling Grace

There's nothing harder than extending grace when we've been wronged, but that's exactly what the Holy Spirit can help us do. He makes it possible for us to offer grace that has nothing to do with the situation at hand.

Spilling grace is the Spirit's work.

A problem had arisen in the ministry. People appeared to have been unjustly handled. I didn't want to go into the space where people I loved and respected were hurting, talking in whispers, frightened—in tears. I needed to have a conversation about that. So as my habit is, I went to the "steps" of my soul and met Him there.

> "Lord God, how do I respond to this atmosphere of fear? This sense of betrayal?"
>
> "Spill grace."
>
> "How do I do that?"
>
> "Be full of the Holy Spirit. He is the Spirit of grace. Stay in touch with the thoughts He brings to mind: the ideas He will give you of touching a hand or saying 'I'm so sorry, what a loss!' 'Would you like a cup of coffee?' 'I'm praying,' 'Want to talk? I'm a good listener—try me!' Offer your heart."
>
> "I can do that. But Lord, when we are at the table face to face and my friend is talking about how she's been treated and I'm hearing things that make me boil or weep, what do I do?"
>
> "Remember, you've only heard one side of the story. I've heard it all. In fact, 'Before a word was spoken, I knew it altogether!' Give people the benefit of the doubt."
>
> "So when I've finished listening to her?"
>
> "Give all parties the benefit of the doubt. Be generous of spirit. It's not your job to judge people's motives. That's My work!"

"They don't sound as if they deserve the benefit of the doubt, Lord—oops, sorry. Er, do I say anything to her about the people in question?"

"If it's full of grace."

"How will I know if what comes out of my mouth is full of grace or is coming from a critical judgmental attitude?"

"You'll know."

"Yes, I suppose I shall! So You're suggesting offering words that someone doesn't really deserve? Something kind, forgiving?"

"I'm not suggesting, Jill!"

"Oops, sorry Lord!"

"Grace gave you what you didn't deserve. Now let that grace spill over."

"But isn't that condoning a wrong?"

"Offer a word of grace that has nothing to do with the situation at hand. Remind your friend of My grace for all people. Say things like, 'You know, often such words are said or deeds happen because there is deep anger or unresolved pain behind the offense. We don't know the motivation. We don't understand the why of the situation yet.'"

"Then what?"

"Focus your conversation on what you *do* know."

"But what do I really know, Lord?"

"That I am God, and I am good—all the time. I am in control even when it seems that all evidence is to the contrary. I have the matter in hand. I am not absent, unaware, or unconcerned about all the tears and heartache. I love you all, both offenders and offended. Start there."

So I invited my crushed friend to coffee, and I did my best to be a true friend. After we had talked for a long time, I heard the Spirit say, "Now it's time to pray."

"What do I pray?"

"That your friend responds with grace to the situation as God would have her respond. Grace in word and action. Grace offered when grace has been offended. Grace knows how to handle offense. He does it all the time!"

The unfairness of it all rose up inside me. "But why should she, Lord? Those people should be spilling grace over her and not expunging her character! It's not fair."

"Right, that's what grace is for—when life isn't fair!"

"Well, they should do it first!"

"Let there be a race. A race to trust Me, to obey Me. I know the heart of the matter, most thoroughly. I know all the whys and wherefores. I have a plan to bless and not to harm. Tell your friend to kneel down in her heart before Me. You come too—right here, right now. Praise Me."

"But how can we praise You for a wrong thing?"

"I'm not asking for your praise for a wrong thing—not for *it* but for Me!"

"Oh."

"When you can't praise Me for what I allow, praise Me for who I am in the midst of what I allow!"

I remembered that He had said to me at another time in a similar situation, "When you're lost for words, it helps to borrow others' words." So my friend and I followed His advice (good move) and used His servant David's words: "'Search me, God, and know my heart; test me and know my anxious thoughts. See if there is any offensive way in me, and lead me in the way everlasting'" (Ps. 139:23–24).

So there at the table, we walked right into the throne room. And we worshiped the One who has "borne our griefs and carried our sorrows" (Isa. 53:4, ESV).

Then we ordered another cup of coffee and talked about the way forward. I listened, amazed, to my friend. She talked of an idea that had come into her head as we had prayed that prayer. An idea about how she could spill grace over the perpetrator of the hurt. It was a great idea, a sweet idea, an "amazing grace" idea! I bowed my head and wondered greatly at the Spirit's work.[2]

Would you like to have a conversation with the Lord too? Where do you need to spill grace? Spend some time journaling your thoughts today.

25

STAYING INVOLVED

Neither old age nor imprisonment stopped Paul from staying actively involved in the affairs of churches and of people far away, and neither of these curtailed his active prayer life that was at once intensely personal and broadly diverse. Staying involved was clearly high on his agenda.

Paul did not sink into lonely despondency in his old age but intentionally went about maintaining healthy, mutually enriching relationships at a deep level with a wide variety of people. He listed ten people by name in his brief letter to Philemon and added to each one a descriptive phrase that shows they were much more than mere acquaintances—they were called "brother," "sister," "fellow soldier," "my son," "fellow prisoner" and "fellow worker." Paul also sent greetings to a whole church of unnamed brothers and sisters.

Although it is not apparent in his letter to Philemon, it is well attested, nevertheless, that Paul also managed to stay informed about the churches scattered across the Roman Empire. He rejoiced when good news was conveyed to him, and he became deeply concerned when he was made aware of sinful behavior in the communities of faith. He spent regular time in prayer so that the work of the Lord in the churches would prosper and individuals would make practical application of the truths they had learned. And from the epistles that have been preserved in the New Testament, we know that Paul maintained an ongoing correspondence with many of the churches he had founded, as well as some that he never visited.

It is also clear in Paul's letters that his interest, concern and involvement were not a one-way street. "Interest, concern and involvement" describes the attitudes and actions of many of the churches toward him as well, and Paul expressed deep appreciation for the encouragement that came his way through their care for him. To Philemon he wrote, "Your love has given me great joy and encouragement, because you, brother, have refreshed the hearts of the Lord's people" (7). Now remember, this was written by an old man in prison. What an encouragement to seniors living in much more congenial circumstances to recognize the possibilities of their own involvement!

Let me give you an example. I have a very good friend who, with his wife, served in a country that was no friend of the Christian faith or of the communities of people who followed Jesus. Despite this, he was welcomed into that country, because, while the people had no time for his faith, they knew he had skills that they desperately needed, so he was *persona grata!* His purpose in being in that difficult situation went much further than wishing to exercise his special skills in that nation, although by doing so he improved the lot of an impoverished people.

My friend's overarching concern was to establish a Christian presence in a godless society. In order to do this, he had to work very hard in his business—not only because he wanted to justify his visa and satisfy the eagle eye of the government that watched him constantly, but also because he felt a moral obligation to do what he had been allowed into the country to do! That became a problem, because as his business boomed, it began to demand more and more of his time, and he had little time left to be the presence he wanted to be. When I visited him in his adopted land, he told me, "I don't know what to do. I can't cope, yet the doors of opportunity are wide open for me to develop the relationships I already enjoy."

At that time I'd been reading Thomas L. Friedman's best-selling book on globalization entitled *The World Is Flat*.[1] Friedman made the point, among many others, that globalization has made the commercial world a more level playing field. One of the reasons for this is the huge network of fiber-optic cables that was laid around the world during the IT boom. This revolutionized communications in many fields. For example, if someone has an MRI in a hospital in Chicago on Thursday afternoon, the data is transferred to India overnight where it is read by an Indian radiologist during his day. The radiologist then sends his findings back to Chicago, where they arrive on the desk of the American doctor on Friday morning, and the person receives a diagnosis within hours of the procedure. What does this have to do with my friend's dilemma? A lot.

I envisioned a healthy, vigorous, highly experienced American Christian businessman living in the suburbs and wondering what to do with himself during his retirement. I suggested to my frazzled friend overseas that he could possibly establish a relationship/partnership with such a retiree in the United States. The retiree could make a brief visit to my friend's far-off land, quickly get a grip on his business operation, return home and take the burden of the management responsibilities off my friend's shoulders. The business part of the operations could be run from the suburban home, and the two could stay in constant touch through the miracles of modern cyberspace. Then my friend could develop the personal relationships far, far away. This arrangement would, in all probability, enhance the quality of the business operation and give the retiree a new lease on life—and we would have a *win, win, win.*

In addition, as the retiree businessman's interest in the ministry of his friend would inevitably grow, he could make occasional trips over to check on the business in person and to give a couple of lectures on business ethics. While doing that, he would allow those who have never related to a believing businessman to learn from his expertise and, more significantly, observe his faith life in action.

If this kind of networking sounds a little over the top, let me remind you of the "network" that Paul was running from prison without cyberspace and fiber-optic cables. At the end of his second letter to Timothy, he wrote about Demas deserting to Thessalonica, Crescens leaving to Galatia, and Titus going to Dalmatia. Luke was still with him, Timothy was en route to him through Troas, and he had sent Tychicus to Ephesus. Then he added that Erastus had stayed on in Corinth, and Trophimus was left sick in Miletus.

Remember, the world is flat now, so it is not such an up-hill task to reach around the world. In fact, it can be done with remarkable ease and efficiency from the comfort of our own homes—even, if necessary, from a wheelchair!

For Personal Reflection and Group Discussion

Points to Ponder

- Imprisonment did not stop Paul from staying actively involved in the affairs of churches and of people far away. Staying involved was clearly high on his agenda.
- Paul also managed to stay informed about the churches scattered across the Roman Empire. His interest, concern and involvement were not a one-way street. "Interest, concern and involvement" describes the attitudes and actions of many of the churches toward him as well.
- Remember, the world is flat now, so it is not such an uphill task to reach around the world. In fact, it can be done with remarkable ease and efficiency from the comfort of our own homes—even, if necessary, from a wheelchair!

Discuss/Journal/Pray

1. Spend some time reflecting on the Points to Ponder.
2. Discuss how Paul was able to keep in touch with people and churches in his day.

3. Discuss ways in which retired people could use modern communications from their homes to partner with brothers and sisters working overseas.

4. How can you stay involved as you age?

A Personal Note from Jill

This lesson ended with the thought that it is possible to minister to people "from the comfort of our own homes—even, if necessary, from a wheelchair!" Let me tell you about my friend Larry, who is confined to a wheelchair, having broken his neck in an industrial accident that left him paralyzed from the neck down.

As Larry lay on life support in ICU, believers prayed for him. Eventually he was revived, and people ministered to him. A well-known pastor gave him a signed Bible, and Larry proudly showed it to all who came to his bedside. In fact, he became known as a "Bible person."

One day, a young man who had also been paralyzed, but from a gunshot wound, was brought into the hospital. A social worker said to Larry, "We're not allowed to talk to patients about religion, but this young man needs to hear about Jesus. I'll wheel you in to see him if you'll talk to him." That day Larry's work as an unofficial chaplain began, and it continues to grow. From a wheelchair! Larry is one of our most faithful greeters at church, and whether in church or in the hospital or at home, Larry ministers to everyone who crosses his path.

26

AUTHENTICITY

Older people find many things hard to take about the younger generation, and vice versa; so like oil and water, the two don't mix. But in my experience, many young people are eager to be in the presence of older people. They love to hear their stories, they find from them genuine answers to their own questions, and if you ask them what they respect most about older people, they'll tell you, "Authenticity!" Experienced men and women who have been on the road a while can provide it, display it and share it. Authenticity is desperately needed, and a study of the aged Paul in action provides a clear picture of what this quality looks like.

I mentioned Paul's second letter to Timothy in the previous chapter when I referenced Paul's involvement in the lives of many people in widely diverse situations. An approximately four-year interval took place between Paul's letter to Philemon and the one to Timothy. Both were written from prison, but it would be a mistake to assume that the apostle had been in the same prison the whole time. Note that the letter to Philemon ends with Paul writing, "One thing more: Prepare a guest room for me, because I hope to be restored to you in answer to your prayers" (Philem. 22). Was this hope realized, or was Paul sentenced to spend the rest of his days in a prison cell?

There is good reason to believe that Paul was actually released from prison and immediately embarked on further ministry. For example, we believe that he later spent time with Titus in Crete. He wrote, "The reason I left you in Crete was that you might put in order what was left unfinished and appoint elders in every town, as I directed you" (Titus 1:5). But in the Acts of the Apostles, we have no record of what apparently was a significant ministry in this Mediterranean island. Moreover, when Paul tried to explain the extent of his ministry to the Romans, who were not familiar with him, he wrote, "From Jerusalem all the way around to Illyricum [modern-day Albania], I have fully proclaimed the gospel of Christ" (Rom. 15:19). There is no mention of this journey in Acts. So it is reasonable to conclude that Paul was in fact released from prison after writing to Philemon but was arrested again later and reimprisoned.

However the details played out, Paul spent the intervening years between his prison terms in active, fruitful work. It was during the second imprisonment, obviously aware that his days were numbered, that he wrote to Timothy. He was now four years older and still going strong, but he was aware that "the time of [his] departure [had] come" (2 Tim. 4:6, ESV).

If we are right in thinking that Paul did actually set off on further ministry travels and challenges upon being released from prison, this speaks volumes about the resilience, determination, dedication and enthusiasm of the old man! And it encourages all of us to keep on keeping on.

AUTHENTICITY

A friend of mine who lives in St. Petersburg, Russia, tells of his grandfather, a pastor during the Soviet regime, who was imprisoned for his Christian activities. His grandfather's health dramatically deteriorated in prison, and after many years there, he was released with strict instructions not to resume his ministry activities. Upon his return home, there was great rejoicing in the church community from which he had been separated for so long.

During the pastor's absence, many people had come to faith in Christ; but in the denomination in which he served, he alone was authorized to conduct baptismal services. On inquiry, he discovered that literally hundreds were waiting for an authorized person to baptize them. So he ordered the ice on the lake to be broken; and the old man, sick and weak from years in prison, waded into the frigid water and singlehandedly baptized the new believers. He was returned immediately to his sickbed, and within days he was arrested and imprisoned once again. He died shortly thereafter. The story of the church worldwide is replete with stories of such courage, resilience, and a never-say-die spirit of service and sacrifice.

Note that in his instructions to Titus, Paul wrote details as to the kind of teaching the young minister must bring to the people under his charge. For example, "You . . . must teach what is appropriate to sound doctrine. Teach the older men to be temperate, worthy of respect, self-controlled, and sound in faith, in love and in endurance" (Titus 2:1–2). I am inclined to believe that when Titus read these words out to the old men in Crete, they listened carefully because they knew the man who had written them. He was authentic, he was credible, and his example was exemplary. They had, no doubt, seen Paul in action during his time in Crete; and now that he was back in prison, they knew that he was exemplifying the characteristics that he wanted to see in these older men in the church.

When Paul spoke, people listened. Few things are as compelling as words spoken by someone who has a track record of practicing what he preaches. We can't demand respect, but we can gain it by being authentic. That is what Paul looked for—men who were "worthy of respect."

For Personal Reflection and Group Discussion

Points to Ponder

- If Paul did actually set off on further missionary travels and challenges after being released from prison, this speaks volumes about the resilience, determination, dedication and enthusiasm of the old man! And it encourages all of us to keep on keeping on.
- Paul wrote to Titus, "Teach the older men to be temperate, worthy of respect, self-controlled, and sound in faith, in love and in endurance" (Titus 2:1–2).
- Paul was authentic, he was credible, and his example was exemplary.
- Few things are as compelling as words spoken by someone who has a track record of practicing what he preaches. We can't demand respect, but we can gain it by being authentic.

AUTHENTICITY

Discuss/Journal/Pray

1. To "keep on keeping on" is far from easy. What things help you endure and persist? What circumstances drain your energy, desires and will to continue?
2. Modern young people claim that they are looking for authenticity. How are older people able to describe and demonstrate authenticity to the younger people in their sphere of influence?
3. In what areas do you need to be more authentic? Pray about it.

A Personal Note from Jill

Read Second Timothy 3:10–17. Note that Paul wrote about his "teaching" and his "way of life." He knew that the authentic person is the one who walks the walk and talks the talk. Take a deeper look into this passage, and look for ways that Paul acted out what he taught. What are some ways that you can do a better job of walking the talk? Pray about that.

27

THE FUNNY SIDE

S peaking of the things young people like in old people, let me tell you about an experience I had many years ago. I met a young pastor who had been converted out of a lifestyle far from God. He shared his new discoveries about Christ with his friends, who themselves came to faith because of what they saw in him. Soon there was quite a band of new believers. To cut a long story short, they planted a church full of young people like themselves! This group asked me to help them. At that time I suppose I was in my late forties.

One time, after a meeting with this burgeoning congregation, I went out for a meal with the pastor and his three young sons. While the pastor attended to some business, I was left in the booth with the three rambunctious, young boys, who proceeded to ignore me completely. Such was their ignoring that they began to discuss me as if I was an invisible man. To my surprise, one of them said—and they all agreed—"He was pretty funny for an old guy!" Their characterization of me as "old" was perfectly artless, and I suppose compared to them, I *was* old. But what interested me most, after I got over my wounded pride, was that they were surprised that old folks have fun!

Let me point out something in Paul's letter to Philemon that you may have overlooked in your own reading of the book. When Paul wrote, "I appeal to you for my son Onesimus, who became my son while I was in chains. Formerly he was useless to you, but now he has become useful both to you and to me" (10–11), he was playing with words and displaying quite a sense of humor! Onesimus' name means "useful," so when Paul wrote that "Useful" (literally), who had been "useless," had become "useful," the wordplay was undoubtedly intentional! I am led to believe that Paul, despite his circumstances and the seriousness of the issue he was dealing with, was not averse to introducing a little touch of humor.

Most old-timers, those of my acquaintance anyway, retain a sense of humor. They know that life is full of ironies that can be hurtful and disappointing, but they choose to see the funny side. They'll tell people, "Since I've lived so long and learned so much, I'm full of answers. But no one asks me questions anymore!" Then they laugh quietly—and wistfully! Their humor is often self-deprecating as it refers to their waning abilities due to their advancing years. An old lady was pulled over by a policeman who asked her, "Do you know how fast you were traveling?"

"Oh no," she replied, "but it was very fast. You need to understand, young man, that we older people have to drive very fast before we forget where we are going."

Older people no longer need to prove how smart they are or how successful they are becoming. They are not bent on impressing others. They no longer see the need to cover their mistakes and pin the blame on other people. They no longer compete; they aren't even in the game! They are free to be frank about their failings and their faux pas, and they don't hesitate to tell others about them. They laugh at themselves, and their friends join in.

Inner peace and tranquility of heart allow people in less-than-ideal circumstances to view their situations somewhat dispassionately. They look at things that easily trouble other people through a context that reveals such things as passing and therefore of limited significance. "This too shall pass," they remind themselves, giving themselves the chance to note the ironies, incongruities and inconsistencies that abound in everyday life. The irony of "Useful" having been so useless and then becoming so useful was not wasted on Paul. He liked that and thought that Philemon would too! Twenty centuries later we can still see the joke—although knowing a little Greek helps!

I did say that the humor of old people is often self-deprecating—but not always. On one occasion, I was invited to speak to a gathering of senior people, and a little white-haired lady was given the task of introducing me. She made her way laboriously to the podium and in a shaky voice said, "Our speaker today, Stuart Briscoe, needs no introduction, so he won't get one." She then turned on her heel and made her arthritic exit to howls of delight from the old folks! I think Paul himself would at least have smiled in appreciation.

My dear friend Al Sanders has always been one of the funniest people I know, and his wit has not diminished one iota now that he is well advanced in years. Recently he wrote to me and told me that he was finally writing a book. He had not progressed very far, he added, but he had settled on his title (presumably based on the well-known Psalm 90:12, which says, "Teach us to number our days, that we may gain a heart of wisdom"). The title he had chosen? *I'm Trying to Number My Days, But I Keep Losing Count.* Typical humor of the aged—quiet, inoffensive, gentle, unpretentious and therapeutic!

For Personal Reflection and Group Discussion

Points to Ponder

- The boys I listened to were surprised that old folks have fun.
- Most old-timers, in my experience, retain a sense of humor. They know that life is full of ironies that can be hurtful and disappointing, but they choose to see the funny side.
- Older people no longer need to prove how smart they are or how successful they are becoming. They are not bent on impressing others. They are free to be frank about their failings and their faux pas, and they don't hesitate to tell others about them. They laugh at themselves, and their friends join in.
- Typical humor of the aged is quiet, inoffensive, gentle, unpretentious and therapeutic!

Discuss/Journal/Pray

1. Spend some time reflecting on the Points to Ponder.
2. Older people frequently display a willingness to laugh—and have no problem laughing at themselves!

How does laughing at yourself make life so much more pleasant, especially in tough times?

3. How can having a sense of humor help you improve with age?
4. How is humor and the funny side of life therapeutic?
5. Think about something that recently made you laugh. Share it.

A Personal Note from Jill

I like the following story that I wrote for the magazine *Just Between Us*:

> The question, "Are we having fun yet?" is one my husband, Stuart, has asked me hundreds of times in my life! Usually in the most exhausting and un-fun situations!
>
> Stuart's question always makes me laugh. Seeing the funny side of life that sometimes is no fun at all, is where we have found our "funnest" (no such word, but it says what I mean) moments.
>
> Stuart's question also makes me realize that looking at life with a view of being able to laugh at something in the situation or at myself settles me down when I'm uptight. It relaxes me in dark days, helping me to create my own down times wherever I am, whether at home or traveling on my own in the big wide world.
>
> Recently we were going on a walk. Stuart was teasing me about something, and we started to laugh. We ended up laughing for a mile! As we were rounding the bend near our house, Stuart looked at me and said, "There's one great thing (among many others!) about our marriage, Jill—we do have *fun!*" We were not on

a beach, on an exotic trip, or playing golf! We were simply walking around the block near our house on a freezing morning after Stuart had just gotten out of hospital (he's fine!) and I had just gotten back from a week in prison (I'm fine!), where I had been speaking to life-termers. We had problems galore in our lives (in fact, some of those problems had put their Nikes on and chosen to accompany us on our walk), but here we were having so much fun!

I have also learned that I can have a lot of fun by laughing at life and at myself! That, of course, is because I am really rather funny! "Never take yourself too seriously," Stuart warned me years ago when we got into ministry. He didn't mean not to take the work of the Lord too seriously—doing that is a given—but rather not to take myself too seriously! We really are pretty amusing folks, you know! . . .

Then of course there have been more mundane moments, like when I shut up the house and went shopping, having left the upstairs bathroom sink blocked with the tap running. It wasn't much fun coming home to a downpour through the kitchen ceiling that was sagging alarmingly! (Stuart, of course, was away!) It took a while that time for me to laugh at myself. The police and firemen thought it was funny immediately and helped me to see the humor after a bit! But I know that when there's nothing to laugh at outside myself, there will always be something to poke fun at inside myself! . . .

Real joy has to do with the joy of the Lord, which He shares with us when things are not always easy. It is sensing God's delight (see Zeph. 3:17) in our hearts!

So, wherever God places you, whether in good circumstances or difficult ones, grab on to the funny side of life, and learn to laugh at yourself. In the process you might just discover that you are not only having fun, but more importantly, you've found the joy of the Lord.[1]

PART THREE

AGING: OLDER PEOPLE IN THE CONTEMPORARY CHURCH

*Those who are planted in the house of the L*ORD *shall flourish in the courts of our God. They shall still bear fruit in old age; they shall be fresh and flourishing.*

Psalm 92:13–14, NKJV

While many churches are transitioning to new models of "doing church," none seem to be doing so at the expense of youth. Surely we have missed the Bible's emphasis on honoring age.

—Tim Challies

28

SENIORS IN THE CHURCH

Most towns in England, both small and large, have a Main Street and a Church Street. The latter, as its name implies, is frequently the home of churches representing main denominations and other nonaffiliated fellowships. I'm sure that the sight of church after church standing in line must cause some people to assume that Christians don't get along with each other. There's much more to our many denominations than that, as those inside the churches know full well, but we do need to be aware of the image we portray to a curious and skeptical world.

A midsized industrial town in the north of England, with which I am well acquainted, suffered a serious economic decline. It was reflected the length of Main Street in boarded-up shops and abandoned warehouses. On Church Street, which included no less than three Methodist churches within a few hundred yards of each other, the buildings were in better condition. Still, the United Methodist Church, the Primitive Methodist Church and the Wesleyan Methodist Church were all barely keeping their noses above water. Each of their congregations consisted of a handful of elderly people, most of whom had attended their respective church since infancy. Noble attempts had been made over the years to amalgamate the three churches; but differences in church polity, special traditions and theological interpretations had always won the day, so the three churches struggled on. The churches diminished as the faithful passed on to their rewards; the decaying buildings awaited either the wrecker's ball or the developer's renaissance.

The faithfulness of these believers, their dogged refusal to yield to modernity and their insistence on perpetuating the vision of the founders of their tradition (as they understood it) were all highly commendable. We need more faithfulness, doggedness, and a healthy sense of history and tradition both inside and outside the church. But as my mother constantly reminded me in my formative years, "Stuart, you can have too much of a good thing." (This motherly reminder was usually administered when I wanted something that seemed perfectly reasonable to me and could see little possibility of it being provided in abundance.) In principle, my mother was right—as I gladly acknowledged about fifty years later. Doggedness can become obduracy, faithfulness can become misplaced, and the backward look of history can obscure a forward vision of the future. We need to recognize that the world we live in is changing, that new problems require attention, that fresh opportunities beckon, that old errors can still be corrected, and that startling new insights are not all wrong!

During my senior-pastor days at Elmbrook Church in Milwaukee, Wisconsin, our congregation intentionally planted new churches around the metropolitan Milwaukee area. Over a number of years, one of these church plants, which met in a rented school, showed significant growth. Slowly and steadily ministries were developed, and the area around this church became aware of a healthy, vibrant fellowship of believers in their midst. Eventually, as is often the case, the church began to outgrow its facilities; and the leadership became aware of Winston Churchill's adage, "We shape our buildings; afterwards our buildings shape us." The problem was, they had nowhere to go!

A mile or two from where the church was meeting was a church facility in beautiful condition that was the home of a rapidly aging and diminishing congregation. Their plight was so severe that they were facing bankruptcy, but the senior citizens in that dying church were not prepared to see their community of faith disappear. Neither were they ready to sell the building that they cherished to someone who would turn it into an automobile showroom, a restaurant or an antique shop. The aging congregants urged their elders to surprise the newer congregation, which needed more space, with a proposal: "If you will take over our mortgage, we will deed the property to you; and, if we may, we would like to join your congregation." Profitable discussions ensued, and it didn't take long before complete agreement had been reached. With relief, one congregation deeded over their treasured property, while the other congregation accepted an incredible gift with joy. The two congregations merged, the newly amalgamated church took on a new life, and the group almost immediately had to have multiple services in the new facility. It can be done!

Another of our church plants ran into a problem about two years into its existence. Among other things, there were points of contention relating to differing generational views on church order and worship. An ugly church split ensued; half the congregation packed their bags and left. Families were torn apart, long-standing friendships were damaged, and the church's reputation in the community took a major hit. The group that left the church started another church a mile or two down the road. Both churches slowly began to grow in numbers and, if not immediately then certainly eventually, in grace. Time is a great healer. Many of the original, discontented people from the split had problems in the new church they founded, so they moved on once again. A new pastor took over, and he promptly contacted the church from which his church had parted and suggested a reconciliation. Meetings took place, issues were addressed, confessions were made, apologies were offered and accepted, and a public service of reconciliation was advertised and held. God was honored, healing began, and the community saw Christians behaving well. In time, the kingdom was extended.

It's hard for older people to let go of the things they have built and the institutions they cherish. They have their comfort zones and their fears, they hold tightly to their traditions, and they treasure their memories. But they also face a church life that is changing in the same way that everything else in their lives is changing. So what can be done?

The older people—the ones whose vision birthed the church, whose loving sacrificial involvement nurtured and developed the church, and whose money has kept the church afloat through good times and bad—must be considered and not disregarded. Their views must be acknowledged, not ignored. They must be helped through changes, cherished through upheavals and affirmed through turmoil. Above all else, they must be cared for by the community of faith. When this is done, there is a much greater chance that harmony will prevail and that much potential heartache will be avoided. In addition, the older folks will be more likely to cooperate in the necessary changes. But this is only half the story!

For Personal Reflection and Group Discussion

Points to Ponder

- Churches that act independently of each other convey a message to unbelievers that Christians have a hard time getting along with one another. We do need to be aware of the image we portray.
- We need more faithfulness, doggedness, and a healthy sense of history and tradition both inside and outside the church.
- Doggedness can become obduracy, faithfulness can become misplaced, and the backward look of history can obscure a forward vision of the future.
- It's hard for older people to let go of the things they have built and the institutions they cherish. But they face a church life that is changing in the same way everything else is changing.

Discuss/Journal/Pray

1. Spend some time reflecting on the Points to Ponder.

2. Local churches are not without their problems, and seniors frequently find their lives unsettled by the ongoing changes in their church. Why not gather together a group of church leadership and seniors to discuss the chapters in part 3 of this book to help them better understand and learn the needs of seniors in their church(es)?

3. Before discussing differences in the church, think about the things that all believers have in common (see Eph. 4:1–7). Make a list.

4. How can an interest in history obscure a vision of the future?

5. People are frequently hurt by what takes place in church life. Clearly this is wrong, but when it does happen, what steps can we take to bring about healing and blessing?

6. A good place to start the healing process is to pray with close friends who will "speak the truth in love" to us (see Eph. 4:15).

A Personal Note from Jill

I love this story that Stuart likes to tell:

> Jim* was a good, solid citizen, a man of opinions who had a gift for expressing them. He had definite views on worship music—nothing unusual about that! One of the musical groups in our church played a certain style of music that left no one happily neutral. People either loved it or loathed it. The group was

called Bluegrace—no prizes for guessing what type of music. Jim was also one of those men who believed that going to church meant that people dressed up, even though many more thought people should dress down. This did not help Jim's blood pressure. On the relatively rare occasions when Bluegrace participated in the worship, Jim expressed his disapproval by standing up, adjusting his tie, straightening his jacket, and marching briskly out of the building, where he stayed until the "music" ended. He then returned and resumed his worship.

This went on for some time, until one day Jim asked to talk to me. He said, "Stuart, I've been reading Isaiah, and he talked about how our righteousness is like filthy rags." I nodded and wondered where he was going with this conversation. He went on, "You know I can't stand Bluegrace, and I've been walking out whenever they lead worship. I have been self-righteous, and God thinks that my self-righteousness is like filthy rags. You'll never see that behavior from me again. I'm going to ask all those young men to forgive my attitude."

I replied, "That's great, Jim. That's the kind of attitude we all need. Go and talk to those young guys, and tell them one thing from me: ask them to turn down the volume!"

Jim replied with a grin. "I'll say amen to that!"

*Name changed

Why not take a younger person out for coffee and discuss the challenges of growing older in a younger world? As you talk, really listen to each other!

29

MARGINALIZED AND TRAUMATIZED

Almost twenty years ago, Jill and I were invited to address a gathering of a few hundred seniors at a weekend conference in North Carolina. The majority of the people in attendance were retired, still in good health, full of ideas, bursting with experience, capable and accomplished. "But," they said, "in our churches we are being marginalized. They don't need us, they don't want us, they won't listen to us, they disregard us."

It's worth noting that these were not professional grumblers. They were the visionaries, the givers, the workers, the prayers and the leaders who had been God's means of either bringing the churches in question into being or to their present position of significance. Yet at some point in their aging, these mature saints had been deemed redundant. In between our teaching sessions, we heard lots of stories, saw many tears shed and tried to answer many questions from troubled hearts. Both of us came away from the conference deeply concerned. Marginalization in the church is a scandal.

In addition to speaking frequently about being marginalized, the conferees confessed to being traumatized. They were referring not to their church lives but to their daily living situations. Frankly, many were worried about the dangerous uncertainties of international affairs and the apparent inability of politicians in Washington to effectively address the issues facing the nation. They were troubled by the trends in society in general, in which "human rights" are emphasized at the expense of human responsibilities, leading to the legalization of behaviors that flatly contradict divine principles. They were worried as well about the incidence of divorce among their children and the resultant upheaval in their own lives and their grandchildren's upbringing. Those who had grandchildren in their twenties fretted about them leaving the church; they feared this was the first step to them leaving the faith, and they despaired of being able to do anything about it.

Financial matters rested heavily upon them too. Some of them, recently retired, had discovered that they couldn't afford to be retired, and they were actually looking for employment. Still others had been let go by companies that they had served for more than thirty years.

Added to all this, a number spoke of their failing health, although it must be said that the majority of them looked to be in far better shape than their parents would have been at the same age! And not a few of them were clearly mourning the loss of beloved life partners and were trying to adjust to life on their own.

The weekend in North Carolina opened my eyes to the numbers of seniors in our society and in our churches and to the particular struggles that many of them experience. On returning to my home church, I began to explore how exactly we were ministering to the seniors in our church family. I asked one of the pastoral staff—a gifted woman who had many years of experience as a nurse and was now distinguishing herself in children's ministries—to find out how many seniors we had in our church and what exactly we were doing with and for them. It didn't take her long to return with two answers, both of which were challenging. She told me, "We have one thousand seniors listed in our computerized mailing list, and we're doing very little specifically for them." I then asked her to contact megachurches similar to ours to see what they could tell us. The message we heard from them was similar to what we had discovered in our own fellowship—they had large numbers of seniors in attendance, but little was being done to address the two big problems of marginalization and traumatization.

We decided that something ought to be done, so we took it a stage further and actually did something! With the agreement of the church elders, I asked the children's pastor who had done the research to switch from children's ministries to seniors' ministries. (I had discovered that her nursing career had included a long stint serving as a liaison between the hospital and surgical patients being released to home care. Her job was to work with the families—often of aging patients—to ensure that they were well cared for. She understood aging, suffering and care—she was ready-made for seniors' ministry!)

Armed with her computerized list of one thousand seniors, this woman went looking for the seniors. She promptly ran into a problem. Remember, AARP says that fifty-five-year-olds are now seniors, despite their vehement denials.

We were quickly made aware that the younger seniors didn't want to be in the same ministry as their parents! That's right; you heard it correctly! We should have known that there is little similarity between a healthy senior in his late fifties to midseventies and his aging mother in her mideighties to early nineties. Our newly minted seniors' ministry was divided into two before it had barely become one!

Our new seniors' ministries pastor quickly informed me that when she interviewed the brothers and sisters to whom she would minister, they were more than ready to talk. She simply asked them, "Would you tell me your story?" They gladly shared about their upbringing and spiritual pilgrimage. They were open about their problems and frank about their needs. Many spoke of broken dreams and others told of lives lived well. They were ready to state their objections too—concerning any and every topic! But above all, they were eager to tackle marginalization and traumatization.

First—and this became the dominant characteristic of these new ministries—these seniors had to pray, and they refused to move until the matter at hand had been adequately bathed in prayer! They had been around long enough to learn that we humans, no matter how vigorous and gifted, are limited. This is a lesson that is not always appreciated by younger people who are full of ambition and energy and who seek the latest models, materials and methods of doing ministry. Our seniors had seen many things billed as "the latest" that had simply failed to last. They had been around the block enough times to know that "fools rush in where angels fear to tread."[1] So they stepped cautiously.

These older Christians may not have known that Robbie Burns, the Scottish poet who was once a plowboy, one day scythed through a fragile nest of field mice. Sadder and wiser, Burns penned that "the best laid schemes of mice and men are apt to go awry" (loosely translated from an incomprehensible Scottish dialect).[2] But these seniors did know from their own experience that their best-laid plans were not necessarily the ways in which God, who, according to the British poet William Cowper, "moves in a mysterious way, His wonders to perform," would accomplish His purposes. Experience had taught them dependence, and that is why they regarded prayer as a "declaration of dependence." We learned a lot from them!

For Personal Reflection and Group Discussion

Points to Ponder

- "In our churches we are being marginalized. They don't need us, they don't want us, they won't listen to us, they disregard us."
- Seniors confessed to being traumatized. They were referring not to their church lives but to their daily living situations.
- We decided that something ought to be done, so we took it a stage further and actually did something!
- Those who became part of our new seniors' ministry refused to move until the matter at hand had been adequately bathed in prayer. They regarded prayer as a "declaration of dependence." We learned a lot from them!

Discuss/Journal/Pray

1. Spend some time reflecting on the Points to Ponder.
2. Is your church situation in any way similar to the one just described?
3. Do you feel marginalized or parked on the sidelines of your church?
4. If, as a senior, you are affirmed and involved in your church, what advice would you give to a brother or sister whose experience is different from yours?
5. It has been said, "When all is said and done, far more is said than done." Do you agree? If so, what action do you think should be taken about the things that concern you?
6. Have your issues been adequately bathed in prayer? Pray about them now.

A Personal Note from Jill

Old Milwaukee, our adopted American home, is famous for more than beer! We do brats too! But come to Milwaukee on a Friday night, and you'll be invited to a fish fry. There you will be plied with all-you-can-eat fish freshly caught in one of our Great Lakes, potato pancakes, applesauce, french fries, pumpernickel bread and a beverage of your choice. You'll usually have to stand in line longer than you want to as well.

Our new seniors' ministry decided that the demand for Friday night fish fries exceeded the supply of Friday night fish fryers. Recognizing the potential of this situation, they prayed—of course! They also recognized that seniors need-ed a fellowship time and that many of their friends needed something to do and especially needed somewhere to go on Friday nights. These friends also needed to be introduced to Christian fellowship and ministry. So our Friday night fish fry was born. It was staffed and organized by seniors, but everybody was invited; and the people of Milwaukee, who love a fish fry, came in the hundreds. The crowd included families, young couples, kids on a date and seniors in their wheelchairs. The format was simple—good food, reasonable prices and profits donated to missions. Lots of lighthearted conversation ensued after the evening's speaker gave a twenty-minute talk. Stuart was the invited speaker on one occasion, and as he stood in line waiting for his fish, he overheard two ladies in conversation in the line behind him: "I'm so glad you came. I only heard about this a couple of weeks ago. But the people here are so friendly, the food is good, the price is right—and I believe that all profits go to charity or something. They have a talk at the end. It's not too long and really quite interesting. In fact, I've learned a lot."

Our seniors had caught the vision, they were being affirmed, their contemporaries were being reached, and families had an event they could share in with enthusiasm.

30

PARKED ON THE SIDELINES

Let's take a look at the issue of marginalization—or being parked on the sidelines of the church.

When Paul told the Galatians, "There is neither Jew nor Gentile, neither slave nor free, nor is there male and female, for you are all one in Christ Jesus" (Gal. 3:28), he was addressing an issue that caused him much concern. The teaching that believers were "all one in Christ Jesus" was not readily accepted in the early days of the church. The reality is that some of the new believers who lived in what is now the region surrounding Ankara, the modern-day capital of Turkey, were Jews, and the rest were Gentiles. Some, of course, were male and others were female. Some were slaves, and some were masters of slaves. In other words, they were divided by racial, gender and social differences. Their differences were obvious, and their differences were important to them. Nothing very new or startling there!

All societies divide easily, with differences commonly trumping commonalities. We find it easiest to mix with our peers and associate with those of a similar social and economic status. There is no point in denying differences, but neither is there any excuse for failing to respect them. The differences we hold dear are certainly not unimportant, but neither are they all-important. Our position in Christ—that is, the relationship that all believers enjoy with Christ—matters more than any difference in the world. Paul described it this way: "There is one body and one Spirit, just as you were called to one hope when you were called; one Lord, one faith, one baptism; one God and Father of all, who is over all and through all and in all" (Eph. 4:4–6). He focuses on oneness—on the unity that God has created through the work of Christ and the Spirit—of which we are often unaware or unheeding.

At the same time, we are called to recognize and encourage our diversity (see 1 Cor. 12:4–6), some aspects of which are divinely ordained, others less so! This means that we should work hard to craft a unity that respects and encourages a diversity that does not fracture unity. As much as many people doubt it, this can be done! In fact, even skeptical secularists who have little time for the church have been known to admit that the Christian church is able to replace barriers with bridges and bring together people who would normally have little to do with each other. When this does indeed happen, it is a thing of wonder and beauty. When this unity is lacking, we must regretfully admit that those who say that "eleven o'clock on Sunday morning is the most segregated hour of the week" sometimes have a point.

You may ask, "What does this have to do with many older believers feeling that they are being pushed aside in their churches?" The short answer is, "A lot." The task of preserving unity and fostering diversity has proven to be too taxing for many churches. Some of them have settled for unity by discouraging or even disallowing diversity. We all know of churches in which everyone looks, sounds, talks and dresses like everyone else. In those churches, those who do not conform get the message that they don't belong in one way or another.

It might be a case of a church catering to seniors who look askance at tattooed, nose-ringed, miniskirted young women escorted by their tattooed, nose-ringed, blue-jeaned boyfriends. Or conversely, a church focused on reaching unchurched, young people might (hopefully gently) let older people know that their methods are outdated, their songs incomprehensible and dull, their liturgy antiquated, their dress off-putting and their teaching irrelevant—effectively, that their day is done.

On the far other end are churches that abandon unity and start different ministries for each interest group. In this case, for instance, a twentysomething group does their own thing on their own, thus sparing seniors from having to adapt to younger preferences and delivering the younger people from having to tolerate tiresome older people's hang-ups. On either end of the spectrum, someone is marginalizing somebody—or perhaps everybody is marginalizing somebody. Since the church today tends to concentrate more on the next generation than on the aging generation, it is the aging who are more often marginalized.

Although they find it painful, some older people remain faithful to their church, but many quietly walk away altogether. Some worship at home, while others abandon the faith. The result is that instead of the church being an example of unity in diversity, it becomes a fractured demonstration of Christians not getting along with each other!

While marginalized seniors need a ministry that caters specifically to their needs and, in some cases, indulges their preferences, they need much more! They need to be part of a community of faith that incorporates people who are totally different from themselves in age, outlook, experience, spiritual development, interests and desires. Non-seniors equally need interaction with those old enough to be their parents and grandparents.

We learned this early in our pastoral ministry. In the heady, exciting days of the Jesus revolution of the late sixties and early seventies, the congregation Jill and I were called to minister to was primarily made up of suburban families. Then all at once, we made contact through one of our church members with a group of about one hundred Jesus people. They were in every way different from the congregation we had been called to serve. Our experience in Europe had taught us that if wild and woolly unchurched young people who were professing Christ were untaught and not properly discipled, they would branch off into all kinds of exotic heresy or worse. On the other hand, if they were integrated into church life, they could become a great power for God. So we welcomed all one hundred of them into the fellowship of about four hundred. On one glorious Sunday morning they all arrived—and the "fun" began!

This is not the place to go into details, but simply put, we knew that the church could have easily split on generational lines at this point. We took preemptive action by teaching about the body of Christ, the diversity of its members, the need for cooperative and complementary relations among generations, and the call to unity in diversity—pointing out that the Trinity is the greatest example of this. We believe that God is three in one—that's diversity in unity. And we also believe that God is one existing in three persons—that's unity in diversity. Anything that God makes resembles the beauty and intricacy of this structure. He made green, but how many greens are there? He designed snowflakes, but how many versions of the same design are there? That was the theology, but most of the people were eager to have some practicality, so we also provided a special seminar called Generation Bridge.

The Generation Bridge seminar was made up of about twenty people who represented different aspects of the church community. They were asked to commit to six weeks together, and they were commissioned to study the epistle of James. The seminar was repeated for those who objected to not having been invited at first. When we announced that it would be offered a third time, we were told, "There's no need; we're getting to know each other and learning to love each other. We don't have issues with each other. In fact, toward the end of the sessions, we older people have been asking the younger ones to explain why they do what they do, and the younger ones are asking for help in understanding their parents!"

Those who came out of the Generation Bridge seminars began to take up positions in the church's life in which they could relate to people on the other side of the bridge, and a cross-fertilization of ministries began. Older people began to work in the children's nursery; younger people started work days in the homes of older single people. Twentysomethings volunteered to pick up older people to transport them to church and to take them shopping afterward.

We also learned that youth provided enthusiasm that seniors sometimes lacked, while seniors provided experience that younger people usually lacked! Enthusiasm without experience breeds chaos; experience without enthusiasm frequently produces stagnation. But enthusiasm wed to experience promises and produces healthy ministries. In other words, ageism—the segregation of communities on the basis of age—is not only wrong; it is dangerously shortsighted and seriously counterproductive! It most definitely has no place in the community of faith.

For Personal Reflection and Group Discussion

Points to Ponder

- All societies divide easily, with differences commonly trumping commonalities. We find it easiest to mix with our peers and associate with those of a similar social and economic status.
- Our position in Christ—that is, the relationship that all believers enjoy with Christ—matters more than any difference in the world. So how do we address our differences?
- We should work hard to craft a unity that respects diversity and to encourage a diversity that does not fracture unity.
- Ageism—the segregation of communities on the basis of age—is not only wrong; it is dangerously shortsighted and seriously counterproductive!

Discuss/Journal/Pray

1. Spend some time reflecting on the Points to Ponder.
2. "The task of preserving unity and fostering diversity has proven to be too taxing for many churches." Discuss how your church handles this major issue.
3. It was stated in this chapter that one extreme reaction to the difficulty of fostering unity is to abandon unity and start different ministries for each interest group, while the other extreme is to create "unity" by discouraging or disallowing diversity. Either way someone is marginalizing someone. How true is this?
4. As we saw above, since the church today often concentrates on the next generation, it is the older people who are more often parked on the sidelines. How might the church prevent this from happening? Why don't you start praying about this for your church?
5. Have you felt as if you have been parked on the sidelines? Pray about that.

A Personal Note from Jill

Stuart tells the following story:

> A middle-aged lady called me one Sunday afternoon and said, "Round about lunch time today, I was driving, and my car got a flat tire. I didn't know what to do. Then a young couple pulled up behind me on the side of the road, changed the tire, and then, on learning that I was alone, took me out for lunch and insisted on paying! They said that they had just been to church and that you had encouraged the congregation to go out and do an act of outrageous kindness today,

and this was their outrageous act. If this is the kind of young people being produced in your church—young people who want to help older people—I'd like to join your church. May I?"

All of us, myself included, need to practice seeing opportunities in our daily doings. It can and must be done!

31

TAMING THE TRAUMA

Hillary Clinton, former secretary of state and presidential candidate, was asked by an interviewer, "When you heard about your husband's affair with a White House intern, how did you react?" Probably expecting the question, she replied immediately, "I wanted to stay in bed, pull the covers over my head and have a nervous breakdown. But I didn't have time!" No doubt Mrs. Clinton was traumatized by the news, but her reaction—as she described it—was quite remarkable. She found strength from somewhere to carry on.

When people are traumatized, they find it easier to pull the covers over their heads than to get up and carry on with lives of purpose and conviction. Many in the process of aging are finding their lives increasingly loaded with events and situations that cause them great pain and fear, which tend to drag them down into depression and despair and lead them to resigned withdrawal.

The workers in any ministry for the aging must be aware of the traumatization of aging believers. Older people who testify to being traumatized by world events and societal changes are convinced that things are not the way they ought to be. Ask them, and they'll tell you so, and they may well be right more often than they're wrong. But if their focus is on what's wrong with the world in general and with their part of the world in particular, their vision is desperately in need of an overhaul. An appropriate ministry of up-building and encouragement is called for!

This ministry should take at least two forms. First, the regular exposition of Scripture for the whole body of believers of all ages should constantly remind the congregation of what God is doing in the world today. The grand narrative of God's purposes recorded in Scripture must be taught in its fullness—starting with the glories of creation, noting the tragedy of the Fall and all its nefarious consequences, leading to the divine intervention of redemption through Christ (the rolling back of the Fall's consequences wherever found), and culminating with the ultimate consummation of the glory (the new heavens and the new earth). People need to be reminded of the relentless, triumphant march of God's kingdom toward this divinely ordained consummation. They must learn to focus on the last chapter in the grand narrative of God's eternal purposes as revealed in Scripture. They must be reminded that in trusting Christ for salvation, they also pledged allegiance to Him and His purposes, and He is the One who wins in the end. (If you commit to the King, you're committed to His kingdom.)

People also need to be assured that as they have pledged allegiance to Christ, He has pledged allegiance to them. They can say with Paul, "I know whom I have believed, and am convinced that he is able to guard what I have entrusted to him until that day" (2 Tim. 1:12). As they are still here on earth, they have not retired as members of the Kingdom, so they need to be actively involved in the grand march of God's eternal purposes. Something of lasting eternal worth is still waiting to be accomplished; otherwise they would already have been transported to glory.

In other words, instead of pulling the covers over their heads, people need to say, "Frankly, when I look at my world and consider my trauma, I'd like to hide from it all, but I don't have time. There's too much to be done." Those who are overcome by life's rough edges and traumatized by life's raw deals need first of all to hear Spirit-anointed preaching of the Word of God in all its life-transforming power and with its offers of abundant grace.

Second, the exposition of Scripture from the pulpit for the whole congregation needs to be supplemented specifically for those who are dealing with traumatic events associated with the aging process. They need practical help, for instance, in facing unwanted unemployment, parenting adult children, raising grandchildren, adjusting to bereavement—in living well as an aging person in a confusing and rapidly changing world. That's a longwinded way of saying that the church needs to offer something like a series of "senior seminars" in which the issues that cause seniors headaches and heart-aches are addressed in the context of the fellowship of faith.

Many of these issues are of such wide interest beyond the church's walls that, if presented carefully, the seminars could become a magnet for unbelievers. Don't forget that unbelievers get traumatized too! For example, how many grandparents would love some instruction on grandparenting, particularly if, for example, they are raising their grandchildren long after they thought their child-raising days were over? What about some lectures on healthcare? Who is not in need of help in finding a way through the thickets of confusing and often conflicting regulations? Only a specialized minority of people find the science of economics anything but dismal, but many would respond to a chance to hear a few politicians debate the economy and to have their questions on the topic answered! It's a rare person who has no interest in money, particularly his or her own, so some instruction on wills would also be well received. ("What will the government do with my money when I'm gone if I die intestate?" or "How can I leave my money to my grandkids so that they can't get at it too soon?") Information on insurance or investments could prove helpful, as long as safeguards against commercial opportunism are built in.

Some people of a more active frame of mind might prefer something more vigorous than a seminar. How about a walking club? A hiking club? A gardening club? A book club? A quilting club? A friend of mine, a chaplain in a retirement community, has a Harley club. He and his numerous riding buddies regularly roar around the countryside with age-defying—and death-defying—abandon. Others who are really slowing down might enjoy a bird-watching club that is considerably more suited to their age. Stamp-collecting, anyone?

Aging people can reasonably expect to find help and support in the community of faith. For this to happen, though, churches need to minister to them in a way that is relevant and compelling. Then, instead of slip-sliding into irrelevance and disappointment, they will continue being built up in their faith so that their lives are still rich, full and fruitful. They need to lay hold of the promises of Psalm 92: "The righteous will flourish like a palm tree, they will grow like a cedar of Lebanon; planted in the house of the LORD, they will flourish in the courts of our God. They will still bear fruit in old age, they will stay fresh and green" (92:12–14). Fresh and green, not dry and dusty!

For Personal Reflection and Group Discussion

Points to Ponder

- Any ministry for those who are aging must be aware of the traumatization of the aging believer. Up-building and encouragement is called for!
- People need to be assured that as they are still here on earth, they have not retired as members of God's kingdom, so they need to be actively involved in the grand march of God's eternal purposes.
- The church needs to offer something like a series of "senior seminars" in which the issues that cause seniors headaches and heartaches are addressed in the context of the fellowship of faith.

Discuss/Journal/Pray

1. Spend some time reflecting on the Points to Ponder.
2. Discuss the topics suggested in this chapter that could be addressed in "senior seminars." Which topics do you think would be most profitable for your church? What other ideas do you have?

3. Make a list of topics, and seek an opportunity to discuss them with your church leaders.

4. Hope springs eternal in the human heart, but for many people hope has lost its spring! If churchgoers are intentional in planning events and offering regular activities, even the most discouraged person can find something to look forward to. Hope can be reborn, especially if the event is led by people of vibrant faith. Pray about this.

A Personal Note from Jill

Having completed a lecture on spiritual gifts, I noticed a woman sitting alone and looking very discouraged. I sat beside her and inquired as to why she looked so forlorn. She responded, "You gave this wonderful talk about gifts and what we should do with them, but I don't have any gifts. I can't speak in public, I can't sing, and I'm no good at counseling people."

So I asked her, "What do you enjoy doing?"

Almost inaudibly she replied, "Crafts."

To her surprise, I enthusiastically responded, "That's wonderful. That's a precious gift. Jesus loves people who do crafts. He was a craftsman Himself. Your gift needs to be used to benefit others. How do you think you could do that?"

This woman was an expert quilter, so starting a quilting club was a natural choice for her! Her neighbors eagerly responded to her invitation to learn quilting. This meant that they regularly sat around a large table for long periods of time, working at their craft and talking! She eventually became more at ease sharing her faith in congenial circumstances, and the good news spread as women learned about quilting—and a whole lot more!

Remember, however old you are, you are worth as much to God as you were when you were young. One of my life lessons is learning that I can still dream. There are still mountains I want to climb and rivers in flood I want to cross just for Him. Like Caleb at the young age of eighty, I find myself saying, "Give me this mountain."

See what I mean? Gifts don't age, and a heart for the Lord can be ever young. My grand and consuming dream—to get a little bit of my lost world to love Him whom I love to distraction—allows me to live in happy denial of my physical weaknesses and spurs me on to higher planes.[1] God thinks that I am worth employing in His kingdom to the end of the race.

Take some time quietly with God and ask Him what gifts He gave you and how He still wants to use them, because remember, spiritual gifts don't age.

32

MOTIVATING AND MOBILIZING

I t's hard to believe, but the baby boomers (those born between 1946 and 1964) are reaching retirement age. That means that they have become seniors, and as they are numerous, they now constitute the fastest-growing segment of the US population. What started out as a boom in babies after "Johnny came marching home" from war in 1945 has now become an unprecedented boom of seniors marching toward the upper echelons of the age brackets—ever upward!

The first boomers reached sixty-five in 2011. Add to this reality the huge increase in life expectancy in recent years, and we see why by the year 2031, "Americans age 65 and older are projected to number 75 million, nearly doubled from 39 million in 2008."[1] The politicians know this reality, and it causes them sleepless nights—although some would say not sleepless enough to spur them to meaningful action as of yet.

If it is common knowledge that the boomers have arrived at "seniorhood" in unprecedented numbers, shouldn't the church also be aware of this demographic phenomenon and take appropriate steps? These seniors are the best-educated generation and are the most experienced in life, business, church and relationships. They have the most discretionary income and free time of all people. They also have had the most opportunities to absorb spiritual truth. By every measurement they should be the most mature, godly, accomplished, blessed people around. In short, they are a vast, rich resource.

While the seniors in the church constitute such a hugely gifted resource, their contemporaries outside the church constitute an even vaster unreached people group. They are also, generally speaking, closest to eternity, and that means that their eternal well-being should be a major concern of the church. It doesn't require an awful lot of thought to recognize that if we're going to reach our generation with the gospel, we must have a realistic ministry of evangelism to the burgeoning masses of retiring boomers. It requires even less thought to recognize that the people best suited to specialize in reaching seniors are the large numbers of seniors in the church. The big question is how.

First of all, we have to deal with those in the church who complain, with varying degrees of justification, that they are being marginalized. They need to be taught the incontrovertible fact that God has certainly not marginalized them. Even a brief study of Scripture will reveal that God has historically worked wonders through older people, and there is no reason to suppose that He has changed His mind on that score. The church may have put the old folks out to grass, but God hasn't! The aging should start grazing the new stretches of grass before them!

Years ago in one of our periods of ministry, Jill felt underutilized because there was no place for her in the organized ministry of which we were a part. Up until that time, she had always been very active in ministry, and it was hard for her not to be using her gifts and energy for the Kingdom. I pointed out to her that around our home were dozens of cottages occupied by older people who never went near a church, and I suggested that she approach them. She began to visit cottage after cottage, befriend the people, and invite them to read and study the Bible in our home. After a year or two of burgeoning ministry, the numbers attending her study far outstripped the capacity of our home to accommodate them. Larger premises had to be found, and the gospel spread among an unreached people group on our doorstep.

As I drove one day in a developing country, I noted with great interest the number of cows, goats and sheep tethered on narrow strips of grass on either side of the road and in the median strips of grass along divided highways. Pastureland was in desperately short supply, so the cattle had learned to graze where they were tethered. Like those animals, I say that we should graze where we're parked, bloom where we're planted, play the hand we're dealt—whatever colorful metaphor best describes each situation! That's what Jill did when she felt that she had been parked on the sidelines for a period of her life, and the result was fruitful ministry.

There is a second tendency among older believers that needs to be addressed. It's the tendency to decide, "I've done my bit; now it's the young people's turn." That is partially true, which means that it is not altogether true! It is true that it is the young people's turn, but it is not true that the older people have done their bit. No doubt they have a done a bit of their bit, but that should not be confused with having completed their bit. For one thing, there is too great a need and too many opportunities to allow anyone the privilege of retiring from the fray.

Some of you will remember when President George W. Bush landed in a fixed-wing airplane on the deck of an aircraft carrier during the controversial days of the Iraq War. Wearing a flight suit and carrying a helmet under his arm, he marched across the deck with a banner unfurled behind him that stated "Mission Accomplished." The president later conceded that it had been a mistake to unfurl the banner at that time; the war continued for eight more years!

It's also premature for any Christian to assume that the church's mission has been accomplished or that it can be safely left to the younger people while the older people retire from the conflict. That amounts to unfurling the banner prematurely—a big mistake. The task is far from completed, and the objectives have yet to be accomplished.

Reaching people effectively with the gospel involves three stages:

1. Presence
2. Credibility
3. Communication

I could give many illustrations of friends of mine in their sixties and upward who have grasped and implemented these principles, but I will settle for one that particularly illustrates the first principle! A stalwart in our seniors' ministry spoke up at one of their prayer meetings and said, "I think that we've prayed long enough asking God to open a door for us to minister in the retirement center across the street." This was a surprise, as this woman was one of the greatest prayers in the group of excellent prayers. She went on, "I believe that God has given us the answer. The management of the retirement home will not grant us permission to minister on the premises, but he will not refuse our application to move in. So I think that some of us who are talking about downsizing should sell our houses and move in!"

A number of them did just that, thereby establishing a legitimate presence among the people they wanted to bless. At the risk of confusing the issue, let me remind you of the analogy Jesus used. He talked about making His disciples into fishers of men. I doubt very much that Jesus had to teach Peter and his friends the first basic rule of fishing: go where the fish are. You don't catch fish in a swimming pool. Those who wish to catch fish need to take seriously what is involved in going where the fish are—establishing a presence among those to whom we are called to minister. It can be challenging, uncomfortable, threatening and all-too-easily avoided, but it is vital nevertheless. It means that we go where the people are, which is not necessarily where we might prefer to be!

Once we have established a presence, what do we do? Just sit there? No! We need to establish credibility. Unfortunately, Christians in America frequently suffer from bad press. We must confess that much of it is perfectly understandable because of the blatant inconsistencies of too many Christian leaders, but many of the negative attitudes toward Christians stem from moral and ethical positions that Christians espouse and that modern society resists and resents. We have to face the reality that a Christian presence is not always greeted with open arms and cheers of delight.

Because of that, we have to go about establishing credibility among those who may not offer it to us.

One thing is more likely to establish credibility than any other. Tertullian, the Christian apologist, wrote in the first century about Christians living in a hostile society, "It is our care for the helpless, our practice of loving-kindness that brands us in the eyes of many of our opponents. 'Only look,' they say, 'look how they love one another.'"[2] In those days long ago, many criticisms of the early believers were silenced when their opponents saw their good works. Peter said it best: "Live such good lives among the pagans that, though they accuse you of doing wrong, they may see your good works and glorify God on the day he visits us" (1 Pet. 2:12).

Jill and I recently ministered in Malaysia, a predominantly Muslim nation. We were amazed at the depth of involvement of the minority Christian churches in Malaysian society. Visiting their homes for the mentally ill, rehabilitation centers for alcoholics and drug addicts, retirement homes for the elderly whose families could not care for them, orphanages, clinics and schools (including one for autistic children), we saw firsthand how they were earning the right to speak the truth of Jesus with conviction and credibility—and their society was taking note.

We too should take note of what Peter said. He explained that the pagan society's reaction to the Christians' exemplary lifestyle being lived out among them would be more than, "What nice people these Christians are! They are so kind and helpful." Peter said that those who benefited from Christian blessing would be so impacted by what they saw and experienced that they would leave their pagan lifestyle and begin to live for God's glory.

How, we might ask, can this be? The answer is that, coupled with the quality of life we live, a clear message is being proclaimed. The secret of a Christian's life is that Jesus, who died as a sacrifice for sins, rose again and indwells the believer; and it is His grace and power, love and blessing that the pagans see and admire. The message of Christ must be communicated with skill and grace, courage and deep compassion, and to such an extent that even older people who are set in their ways may turn to Christ. All of us, whether seniors or neophytes, need to be actively at work in this ministry. We need to be trained, mobilized and well equipped to talk the walk as we joyfully walk the talk.

Our friends who moved into the retirement center across the street from our church were not involved with people at such a dramatic level as our friends in Malaysia, but they were also earning the right to speak the truth in love. This, in principle, is what we need to be doing—mobilizing the gifted seniors in our midst to reach out to the uncommitted seniors on our periphery.

For Personal Reflection and Group Discussion

Points to Ponder

- The baby boomers are reaching retirement age. Seniors constitute the fastest-growing segment of the US population. Any church concerned with evangelizing their contemporaries must therefore consider ways to reach the vast numbers of seniors on their doorsteps.

- Seniors are the best-educated generation and are the most experienced in life, business, church and relationships. By every measurement they should be the most mature, godly, accomplished, blessed people around—a rich resource.
- The church may have put old folks out to grass, but God hasn't! Graze where you're parked; bloom where you're planted; play the hand you're dealt.

Discuss/Journal/Pray

1. Spend some time reflecting on the Points to Ponder.
2. As we noted in this chapter, it's obvious that the people most suited to reaching the retiring boomers with the gospel are the seniors (boomers or otherwise) in the church. The big question is, how?
3. If it is true that effective communication of the gospel involves presence, credibility and communication, what steps do seniors in the church need to take to put themselves in the best positions to reach their contemporaries?
4. Pray about how you can use your gifts and reach out to other seniors around you.

A Personal Note from Jill

Even When

Even when I am old and gray,
do not forsake me, my God,
till I declare your power to the next generation,
your mighty acts to all who are to come.

Psalm 71:18

MOTIVATING AND MOBILIZING

Even when I'm old and gray,
Sun or rain or come what may;
Even when my strength is waning,
Help me, Lord, with knowledge gaining:
Tell the children of Your grace,
Show them how to seek Your face.

Give me inner eyes to see
What You have in mind for me.
Grant me "patient power" to wait
Till I pass through heaven's gate:
Even when I'm old and gray,
Give me strength, Lord, day by day.

Thank you for Your Spirit strong,
Deep within me all day long,
Freshening my thirsty soul,
Strengthening and making whole.
Jesus, may my children see,
Your sweet life controlling me.

Even when I'm old and gray,
I'm resolved to have my say.
Even when they laugh or frown,
I won't let it get me down.
Count on me to tell Your story
Till You take me home to glory!

Even when . . . even when . . . even when.[3]

33

BEYOND IMPROVING

My father was a lay preacher, and my brother and I followed in his footsteps. One day my brother, Bernard, said to me, "Have you ever noticed that when Dad is preaching, he sometimes says, 'Finally,' and other times he says, 'Lastly'?"

"As a matter of fact, I have noticed," I replied. "But have you noticed that when he says 'finally,' he finishes; but when he says 'lastly,' he lasts?" I had to admit that this observation was as astute as it was accurate.

I suppose my father could have defended himself if he had wished by referring to Paul's letter to the Philippians, where he wrote, "Finally, my brothers, rejoice in the Lord," at the end of chapter 2 but then went on for another two chapters (see 3:1, ESV). This reminds me of the golfer who, having missed a tricky short putt, grumbled, "The ball went on a long time after it had stopped."

We've been considering the aging process and have noted that it needs to be recognized as part of the dying that happens to all fallen humanity. This process also has a termination point, and seen in that light, it is an end—the end of earthly existence as we know it, the termination of relationships as we experience them, and the end of awareness of and responsiveness to the world around us. But in another great and glorious sense, it is not the end. We could say that life goes on a long time after it has stopped!

Martha and Mary, two of Jesus' special friends in Bethany, were staring at the bleak exterior of their brother Lazarus' tomb. Four days previously he had passed away. As custom demanded, his corpse had been placed immediately in a tomb and a stone had been rolled over the entrance with a solemn and jarring finality. We don't know how old Lazarus was or how sick he had been, but we do know that he had departed the scene and that his sisters were devastated.

Jesus said to Martha, "I am the resurrection and the life. The one who believes in me will live, even though they die; and whoever lives by believing in me will never die." Then He challenged her with the question, "Do you believe this?" (John 11:25–26). We know that Martha believed what the orthodox Pharisee believed and the Sadducee rejected— namely, that there will be a resurrection at the end of the age. But Jesus' statement went well beyond that. He was not referring to something in the dim and distant future. He was referring to something that was actually going on as He spoke. Lazarus, even though he had died, lived! In fact, he could not die! This was, no doubt, incomprehensible to Martha, so Jesus raised Lazarus from the dead then and there to make the point.

What exactly was the point? If we may say so, the point was that life goes on a long time after it has stopped. Or, if you wish, we might say "finally"—but we are not finished!

But what Jesus said is better: "I am the resurrection and the life." Jesus had at this point not been raised from the dead, but He would be very shortly, and He connected His own resurrection to a new kind of life to be granted and enjoyed by those who followed Him. Later He said to His disciples, "Because I live, you also will live" (John 14:19). Death declares the end of earthly life, but the resurrection of Jesus promises eternal life to the believer. This is the life that those who die enjoy! It is this life that guarantees that the believer will never die eternally even though he or she dies on earth!

New Testament scholar Dr. Leon Morris, commenting on John 11:25–26, wrote, "The moment a man puts his trust in Jesus he begins to experience that life of the age to come which cannot be touched by death. Jesus is bringing Martha a present power, not the promise of a future good."[1]

Notice that Morris said, "The moment a man puts his trust in Jesus he begins to experience that life of the age to come." So think of it! How many years ago did you trust Christ for salvation? Right then you began to experience His life—the life of the age to come. And He has lived in you by His Spirit ever since. "To what end?" you might ask. Paul explained it this way: "We all, who with unveiled faces contemplate the Lord's glory, are being transformed into his image with ever-increasing glory, which comes from the Lord, who is the Spirit" (2 Cor. 3:18). The indwelling Spirit works in the inner recesses of a believer's life to bring about transformation, and the longer this work goes on, the more transformation we can reasonably expect. This is where the improving-with-age principle finds its motivation and power. And there's more!

Do you remember the words of Ecclesiastes about dust going one way and the Spirit going the other way? We should be aware that there's good news about the dust as well as what we have considered concerning the human spirit. Paul told the Roman Christians, "If the Spirit of him who raised Jesus from the dead is living in you, he who raised Christ from the dead will also give life to your mortal bodies because of his Spirit who lives in you" (Rom. 8:11). This promises a bodily resurrection of some kind, which is made even clearer in the letter to the Philippians: "Our citizenship is in heaven. And we eagerly await a Savior from there, the Lord Jesus Christ, who, by the power that enables him to bring everything under his control, will transform our lowly bodies so that they will be like his glorious body" (Phil. 3:20–21). "His glorious body" refers to Christ's resurrection body. His body was recognizable to the disciples, but it was clearly different in a transcendent sense, because it was suited to the eternal realm—to which He ascended in His body! So we also look forward to receiving resurrected bodies ideally suited to the eternal realm to which we will be called when we die.

This will happen when "the creation itself will be liberated from its bondage to decay"—does that sound like outwardly wasting away?—"and brought into the freedom and glory of the children of God" (Rom. 8:21). But there's still more!

John, the aged apostle, told his congregation, "Dear friends, now we are children of God, and what we will be has not yet been made known. But we know that when Christ appears, we shall be like him, for we shall see him as he is" (1 John 3:2). I've never met anyone who claimed to be like

Jesus in every respect. We know that we fall far short of His standards, no matter how deep the work of transformation has been in our lives. Yet the promise is that eventually and finally we will be like Him.

This is what Paul was referring to when he told the Romans, "The hour has already come for you to wake up from your slumber, because our salvation is nearer now than when we first believed" (Rom. 13:11). Some people have been confused by this verse because they thought that their salvation was complete the moment they believed. But in this instance Paul was saying that there are aspects of salvation that we have not experienced and will not experience until we see Jesus. Then and only then will our salvation be complete, and that completion is the ultimate in improving! It is being totally remade to be like Jesus, inhabiting a body ideally suited to "a new heaven and a new earth, where righteousness dwells" (2 Pet. 3:13), which will be our abode for eternity.

This should not surprise us, because God has announced from the throne, "I am making everything new! . . . Write this down, for these words are trustworthy and true" (Rev. 21:5). To make sure that we know what is meant by "everything," John was shown and instructed to record, "Then I saw 'a new heaven and a new earth,' for the first heaven and the first earth had passed away" (21:1).

No more improving with age then for two obvious reasons: First, there will be no such thing as age or aging; that belongs to time, and we're talking eternity! And second, there will be no room for improvement; we can't improve on what God has made completely new! It will all be beyond improving!

For Personal Reflection

Closing Prayer

Dear Lord,

I thank You that in Your eternal purposes, You gave me the gift of life and I was born into this world. Over the years, You have provided for me, taught me and been faithfully concerned about my well-being. I have not always been as close to You as I am called to be. I have not always obeyed You or trusted You as I ought to have done. I confess this and ask for Your forgiveness for the sake of Jesus, Your Son, whose sacrificial death atones for all my sin—in fact, for the sins of the whole world—and offers full and free forgiveness to all who will humbly ask and receive.

As the years have rolled by, I have passed through many stages, but I recognize two things that cannot be denied: One, outwardly I am wasting away. Two, through the gracious work of the Spirit who indwells all who follow Jesus, I can know renewal and refreshment on a daily—no, a moment-by-moment—basis. I can say with the apostle Paul, "Though outwardly we are wasting away, yet inwardly we are being renewed day by day" (2 Cor. 4:16). Thank You, Lord.

I do not know what the future holds or even if I will have much more of an earthly future, but I do believe that my eternal destiny is safe in Your keeping. I look forward to the day when this body that has served me well will also be resurrected and perfected, and I will dwell with You for all eternity in the new heavens and the new earth filled with righteousness. What a prospect! Praise the Lord.

Amen.

BEYOND IMPROVING

A Personal Note from Jill

At Home

*We live by faith, not by sight. We are confident, I say,
and would prefer to be away from the body
and at home with the Lord.*

2 Corinthians 5:7–8

Lord of our lives—our hours and our days
Lord of our years and Lord of our ways,
Lord of our plans, our hopes and our fears
Lord of our destiny, Lord of our tears.
Creator, Provider, Shepherd and King:
Lord of the ages, Your praises we sing.

Savior of sinners risen to be,
Our source of forgiveness, *Redeemer* is He!
Our purpose, our Guide, our *Helper* in strife
The One who transforms us, our true joy in life!
We'll sing songs of Zion though dark is the night
And armed with our faith go forth to the fight.

Healer and Helper bringing relief
To rich man and poor man, beggar and thief.
Spirit of holiness, work in our hearts;
Send us, and spend us, as we do our part.
We will lean on Your shoulder, rely on Your *Word*
And tell our lost world of the things that we've heard.

We'll live in Your *Truth* and speak of Your *Grace*,
We will be Your disciples in time and in space.
Though the road may be lonely and bitter the way,

We'll wait out the night and look for that day
When we're heading for heaven, where "we'll know as
   we're known,"
So we'll stay on the Right Road and see You at Home!

At Home free from heartache, at Home free at last,
Free from the guilt and the shame of the past:
Free from betrayal, and never alone,
Busy in New Earth and close to Your Throne.
Then we shall know *Lord*, and then we shall be
Fitted for Glory for Eternity!
*My child, I am waiting: hurry home, hurry home, hurry
   home!* [2]

NOTES

Introduction

1. Robert Robinson, "Come Thou Fount of Every Blessing," 1757, http://www.sharefaith.com/guide/Christian-Music/hymns-the-songs-and-the-stories/come-thou-fount-of-every-blessing-the-song-and-the-story.html.

Chapter 1: Aging Happens, and You Can't Stop It!

1. Thomas Campbell, *The Oxford Dictionary of Quotations* (Oxford: Oxford University Press, 1941), 187.
2. Jill's adaptation of anonymous poem, "Grandma's Off Her Rocker!" http://www.funnypoets.com/poems/grandmasoffherrocker.htm.

Chapter 2: Aging Means Diminishing

1. Derek Kidner, *The Message of Ecclesiastes* (Downer's Grove: InterVarsity Press, 1976), 13.
2. R.A. Torrey, *How to Work for Christ: A Compendium of Effective Methods* (New York: Revell, 1901).

Chapter 4: Outwardly and Inwardly

1. C.S. Lewis, *The Problem of Pain* (New York: MacMillan, 1962), 83.

Chapter 6: Fresh and Flourishing

1. While other quotations from the NIV in this book come from the NIV's 2011 edition, this rendering of Romans 8:10–11 is taken from the 1984 edition (Holy Bible, New International Version®. Copyright © 1973, 1978, 1984 Biblica. Used by permission of Zondervan. All rights reserved).

Chapter 7: Look Good, Feel Good

1. J.P. Somerville, "King Canute and the Waves," http://faculty.history.wisc.edu/sommerville/123/Canute%20Waves.htm.
2. Jill Briscoe, *Barefoot in My Heart: Starting a Fresh Conversation with God* (Oxford: Monarch, 2011), 94.

Chapter 8: Mirror, Mirror on the Wall

1. Gerhard Kittel, ed., *Theological Dictionary of the New Testament* (Grand Rapids: Eerdmans, 1964), 2:696.
2. See Jill Briscoe, *The Deep Place Where Nobody Goes: Conversations with God on the Steps of My Soul* (Oxford: Monarch, 2005).
3. Jill Briscoe, "Thank You for Your Gift of Life," 2011.

Chapter 9: Jesus Wasn't Elderly

1. John Newton quote found in Cowper and Newton Museum, Olney, Buckinghamshire, England.

Chapter 10: Let's Get Real

1. Isaac Watts, "O God, Our Help in Ages Past," 1719.
2. Jill Briscoe, *God's Front Door: Intimate Conversations with My Lord* (Oxford: Monarch, 2004), 119.

Chapter 11: Shaky Theology

1. Louis Renou, ed., *Hinduism* (New York: George Braziller, 1962), 43.

Chapter 12: The Upside of Aging

1. Adapted from Jill Briscoe, "Staying Green Even as We Gray," 2008, http://www.oneplace.com/ministries/telling-the-truth/read/articles/staying-green-even-as-we-gray-10501.html.

Chapter 13: Free to Be Responsible

1. George Washington's Farewell Address, 1796, http://avalon.law.yale.edu/18th_century/washing.asp.
2. Vitkar E. Frankl, *Man's Search for Meaning* (Boston: Beacon Press, 2006).

Chapter 16: The Joy of Reading

1. James Boswell, *The Life of Samuel Johnson* (New York: Penguin Books, 1979).
2. Paul Tournier, *Learning to Grow Old* (London: SCM, 1972), 32-33.
3. William Shakespeare, *Henry IV, Part 2*, act 3, scene 1.
4. Mark Twain, https://www.goodreads.com/quotes/919-the-man-who-does-not-read-has-no-advantage-over.

Chapter 17: The Best Book

1. Dietrich Bonhoeffer quoted in Richard J. Foster, *Celebration of Discipline: The Path to Spiritual Growth* (San Francisco: Harper & Row, 1978), 29.
2. Eric Metaxas, *Bonhoeffer: Pastor, Martyr, Prophet, Spy* (Nashville: Thomas Nelson, 2011).

Chapter 19: The Next Generation—and the Next

1. Jill Briscoe, "No Greater Joy," 2013.

Chapter 20: Grumpy Old Men

1. Adapted from Win Couchman, "The Grace to Be Diminished," *Just Between Us*, spring 2006, http://justbetweenus.org/pages/page.asp?page_id=86643.

Chapter 21: Hindsight, Insight and Foresight

1. Tournier, *Learning to Grow Old*, 74.

Chapter 22: Alone or Lonely?

1. Mother Teresa, http://www.brainyquote.com/search_results.html?q=loneliness.
2. Foster, *Celebration of Discipline*, 96.
3. William Wordsworth, *Selected Poems* (London: J.M. Dent and Sons Ltd, 1975), 119.
4. Foster, *Celebration of Discipline* (London: Hodder & Stoughton,2008), 97-98.
5. Jill Briscoe, *God's Front Door*, 62–64.

Chapter 23: Paul, the Aged

1. See F. F. Bruce, *Paul: Apostle of the Heart Set Free* (Grand Rapids: Eerdmans, 1977), 399–400.

Chapter 24: Friends: God's Gift to Mankind

1. Neil Postman, *Amusing Ourselves to Death: Public Discourse in the Age of Show Business* (London: Penguin, 1985), 7.

2. Adapted from Jill Briscoe, "Spilling Grace," *Just Between Us* (blog), February 18, 2013, http://blog.justbetweenus. org/2013/02/spilling-grace.html.

Chapter 25: Staying Involved

1.Thomas Friedman, *The World Is Flat* (New York: Farrar, Staus and Giroux, 2005).

Chapter 27: The Funny Side

1. Adapted from Jill Briscoe, "Are We Having Fun Yet?" *Just Between Us*, summer 2006, http://justbetweenus.org/pages/page.asp?page_id=77177.

Chapter 29: Marginalized and Traumatized

1. Alexander Pope, "An Essay on Criticism" in *Oxford Dictionary of Quotations* (Oxford: Oxford Press, 1941), 604:17.
2. Robert Burns, "To a Mouse, on Turning Her Up in Her Nest with the Plough" in *Oxford Dictionary of Quotations*, 172:22.

Chapter 31: Taming the Trauma

1. Portions adapted from Jill Briscoe, "Life Lessons," *Just Between Us*, http://justbetweenus.org/pages/page.asp?page_id=72845.

Chapter 32: Motivating and Mobilizing

1. National Academy of Social Insurance, "How Will Boomers Affect Social Security?" http://www.nasi.org/learn/socialsecurity/boomers.
2. Tertullian quoted in Rodney Stark, *The Rise of Christianity: How the Obscure, Marginal Jesus Movement Became the*

Dominant Religious Force in the Western World in a Few Centuries (New York: Harper Collins, 1997), 87.

3. Jill Briscoe, *Faith Dancing: Conversations in Good Company* (Oxford: Monarch, 2009), 74–75.

Chapter 33: Beyond Improving

1. Dr. Leon Morris, *The Gospel According to John* (Grand Rapids: Eerdmans, 1971), 550.

2. Jill Briscoe, "At Home," 2012.

PUBLICATIONS

Fort Washington, PA 19034

This book is published by CLC Publications, an outreach of CLC Ministries International. The purpose of CLC is to make evangelical Christian literature available to all nations so that people may come to faith and maturity in the Lord Jesus Christ. We hope this book has been life changing and has enriched your walk with God through the work of the Holy Spirit. If you would like to know more about CLC, we invite you to visit our website:

www.clcusa.org

To know more about the remarkable story of the founding of CLC International we encourage you to read

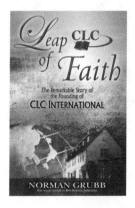

LEAP OF FAITH

Norman Grubb
Paperback
Size 5 1/4 x 8, Pages 248
ISBN: 978-0-87508-650-7
ISBN (*e-book*): 978-1-61958-055-8